Aaron Boyd challenges us to free Jesus from being a captive of our hearts so He can truly shine as "God of this city." Boyd helps us to see our personal links to slavery and poverty and inspires us to become agents of redemption. This book helps us untangle the web of injustice where we find ourselves so we can engage fully in a gospel of freedom.

DAVID BATSTONE
Co-founder and President of the Not For Sale Campaign

This is an amazing song with an amazing story. Every time I hear it and sing it, faith grows in me.

BRENTON BROWN
Christian Musician and Worship Leader

It's not often that an anthem of hope like "God of This City" comes along. I've seen it become a theme all around the world for church leaders and civic leaders alike to bring people together for charging them to take back their communities from the plague of hopelessness their cities face. It rings with the truth that God is still in control and that through Him real change can occur. It's powerful!

EDDIE DEGARMO
President, EMI Christian Music Publishing
Co-creator of the Band DeGarmo and Key

We cannot close our eyes to the pain and suffering that our lack of action has caused in our own backyard. How could we not rescue a generation that has never been given a chance? For the sake of these young silent sons and daughters, *God of This City* is a must-read.

RON LUCE
President and Founder of Teen Mania Ministries
Author of *ReCreate* and *ReCreate Your World*

"God of This City" is much more than simply a worship song. It is also a call to action that echoes God's yearning for "better things yet to come." It powerfully challenges believers to follow Christ in His relentless irresistible pursuit of justice.

PATRICK MCDONALD
Chief Executive of Viva—Together for Children

In *God of This City*, Aaron Boyd and Craig Borlase give us a front-row ticket to their own personal transformation and the transformative power of Christ, but they also invite us to trust God and become much more than spectators or consumers of the wonder and horror going on around us. *God of This City* is a heart-wrenching and hopeful book all at the same time. An inspiring and prophetic book, it is a much-needed breath of hope in a sea of bad news about injustice. The world around us is not the world that must be, nor is it the world that God desires. Aaron and Craig offer the story of their own personal transformation, the transformative power of Christ, and the invitation to become the transformation we so long to see in the world.

R. YORK MOORE
National Evangelist, InterVarsity Christian Fellowship USA

In *God of This City*, Aaron Boyd has captured the very heart of authentic worship: offering ourselves to God as opposed to offering only our words. This expression has led Aaron where I hope it leads many multitudes around the world: to the most broken and hurting.

BENJAMIN NOLOT
Founder and Director of Exodus Cry
Anti-Trafficking Director, International House of Prayer
Kansas City, Missouri

Now and again a song bursts through into the worshipping Church and spreads around the globe quickly. "God of This City" is such a song. It's not always easy to define why certain songs travel so fast around so many different people and nations. Musically and lyrically this is a great song, but what made it connect with people so fast and so deeply? I think one reason is that it mirrors the heart cry of so much of the Church in these days. We long for a breakthrough and to see the greater things that Jesus told us to expect. We long to see the power and compassion of our God impacting our nations, our towns and our cities. This beautiful song from Bluetree helps us rise up in faith, intercede for these things, and look for an awakening.

MATT REDMAN
Songwriter and Worship Leader
Author of *The Unquenchable Worshipper, Facedown* and *Blessed Be Your Name*

It's great when a song stirs up your heart to pray and call on God to visit our towns and cities. I love this song. It makes me want to run into the streets with a "God can save you" placard.

MARTIN SMITH
Songwriter and Singer in the Band Delirious?

We all want to see God move in our families, in our cities and in our nations, but first God must move within our own hearts. In *God of This City*, Aaron Boyd has written a book that will challenge and inspire us all . . . not merely to want change to happen, but also to *be* the change that our world desperately needs. I don't think it will be possible for you to read this book and not be stirred to action.

HOLLY WAGNER
Author of *GodChicks, WarriorChicks* and *GodChicks and the Men They Love*
Co-pastor of The Oasis Church, Los Angeles, California

During the days of the underground railroad, black slaves put the directions and instructions for their escape plots to music called "songs of deliverance." This allowed the slaves to secretly communicate their plan to one another. *God of This City* is like a song of deliverance for everyone who desires to rescue young boys and girls from sex trafficking and slavery. This book is a must-read for everyone who longs to make history "His Story."

KRIS VALLOTTON
Co-founder of Bethel School of Supernatural Ministry
Author of five books, including *The Supernatural Ways of Royalty*
Senior Associate Leader of Bethel Church, Redding, California

GREATER THINGS HAVE YET TO COME

GOD
OF THIS
CITY

aaron boyd + craig borlase

Regal

From Gospel Light
Ventura, California, U.S.A.

Published by Regal
From Gospel Light
Ventura, California, U.S.A.
www.regalbooks.com
Printed in the U.S.A.

Library of Congress Cataloging-in-Publication Data
Boyd, Aaron (Aaron Jordan), 1980-
God of this city : greater things have yet to come / Aaron Boyd, Craig Borlase.
p. cm.
ISBN 978-0-8307-5223-2 (trade paper)
1. Sex—Religious aspects—Christianity. 2. Human trafficking. 3. Church and
social problems. 4. Thailand—Social conditions. I. Borlase, Craig. II. Title.
BT708.B69 2010
261.8'33153—dc22
2010001068

The StandOut International Information Pack is reprinted by permission of
StandOut International. All right reserved.

1 2 3 4 5 6 7 8 9 10 / 17 16 15 14 13 12 11 10

Rights for publishing this book outside the U.S.A. or in non-English languages are
administered by Gospel Light Worldwide, an international not-for-profit ministry.
For additional information, please visit www.glww.org, email info@glww.org, or write
to Gospel Light Worldwide, 1957 Eastman Avenue, Ventura, CA 93003, U.S.A.

CONTENTS

*God of This City is dedicated to the widow, the trafficked girl,
the orphan, the poor, the abused, the ailing, the neglected . . .
to people everywhere who do not have a voice. You are loved. You are
not forgotten. We will stand with you, and together
we will become a voice of hope.*

ACKNOWLEDGMENTS

God of This City is more than a song—it's a call; it's a challenge. This call has challenged and dominated my life for quite some time.

Jill, thank you for believing in me. You never fail to amaze me. You have sacrificed so much to see God demonstrated in our lives. You are an amazing wife and an amazing mum. May I never take you for granted and always tell you how much you mean to me. I love you with every fiber of who I am.

Lily and Josie, you are 4 years and 2 years old at this moment. I am so blessed to have two of the most beautiful, smart, caring and fun girls ever created. You have taught me so much about love.

Andrew and Penny, since day one you have stood by Jill and me. You have laughed and cried with us. You have walked a path of friendship that goes beyond anything any normal person could handle. Thank you.

Tony Patoto, when Andrew and I first met you, we knew we wanted to have you join the ranks. Your guidance and direction are unquestionable. I genuinely cannot express how proud I am to have you as a friend.

PTK and Lisa, you are dreamers and friends. The journey of a thousand miles starts with one step. We have taken that step together. Pete, you bring life to this crazy journey, and you dared to believe that we could change the world. Lisa, thanks for believing in Pete. Alongside every good man there is a great woman.

This journey of Bluetree and Stand Out is only an expression of a life built on relationship. I am blessed to have so many great friends in life. Mum, Dad, Jim, Liz, Jason and Judith, thank you for all your help and support over the years. You are the best role models a person could have. Johnny Hobson, Shiney, Ernie and Comfort, what you guys do blows my mind.

Ding and Joy (Bell, eeeeeeyo!!!), Chalkie, Lynn (all of the Wrights), Griff, Erin, the man that is Tim Mercer, Miyagi Mills, Helen, Michael Jervis, Gradie, Yvone, Liam and the full O'Brian team, Paul and Kathy Mills, Stevie Greer, Vesper guitars, Fender, Gigrig and Zvex, thank you all for your support and help. I couldn't have done this without you guys by my side.

Chris Tomlin, Natalie Grant, Louie Giglio, Matt Redman and everyone else who has not only sung "God of This City" but also taken it as their own call and challenge, thank you.

Craig Borlase, thanks for putting my thoughts and passion into words. Your talent is amazing. And thanks to A. J. Gregory, Steve Lawson and Alanna Swanson for your editorial expertise and commitment to seeing God transform every city.

Jesus. All this stuff has always and will always be about You. You are the beginning and the end. Without You, it's all just noise. To say thank You definitely falls short. My prayer is that You will take these thoughts and stories. Reveal to people that no matter how large the problem or desperate the situation—from brothels in Thailand to earthquakes in Haiti—we already have the answer living within each and every one of us. Until the day we see You in glory, may we never grow weary or faint of telling the world about Your goodness.

INTRODUCTION: INHALE

I'm impatient for change.

I've seen my share of violence and suffering. I spent my childhood in Belfast, Northern Ireland. Mine was a backdrop of bombings, assassinations and acts of terrorism plotted out by the unemployed in local pubs. I wanted that to change. I've watched countless news reports of the problems in the developing world. I've seen the way the camera moves slowly across the feeding lines in African refugee camps, starving bodies that are not quite dead but barely alive. I've wanted that to change too. And I've visited Thailand, where, for the first time, I witnessed the impact of the sexual exploitation of children. I saw how cruel and destructive humans can be, how brutally people can abuse children, how deep the wounds can go. And I want it to change. I want it all to change. The violence, the poverty, the abuse: I want to see our world, our cities, our people transformed for the better.

Impossible? I don't think so. I'm convinced that we can be a part of something that pulls the plug on so much of the injustice, poverty and suffering that surround us.

And here's another thing: It's not just that we *can* be involved; it's that we *have* to be.

That's where faith and music collide. I know that there's something dynamic that happens when we sing. But it's more than words, more than a melody and a drumbeat that transform people. As a worship leader I've always been frustrated with the idea that worship only has to do with a person's heart. This approach can easily lead people to a place where they're just showing up in church on Sundays and singing feel-good songs. All too often people like me who are trying to help lead the church in worship are accused of drawing the church's attention in on itself. Sometimes they're right; we have been guilty of making worship too narrow, too insular, too inward looking. But it doesn't have to be that way. True worship is bigger. True worship means action. It demands that we get involved, that we commit to doing something, to making a difference. Being the change.

When I was younger, we would sing songs about the Catholics. They used to sing about us Protestants too. They were hate-filled tunes—little nursery rhymes with innocent melodies but poisonous lyrics. They tasted sweet but they left our hearts bitter and calloused. The same thing happens when we Christians squeeze our faith into pews on Sunday mornings and leave it there until the next week. We might have the right tunes, melodies and lyrics, but our hearts will grow cold, and our words about how much we love God will be evidence of our hypocrisy. If we sing but don't act, we are at risk of being rendered meaningless.

It's not that singing isn't important. It is. It's vital. But it must not be served solo. For me that means trying to do more than sing about hope and change and the potential within us all to build a better world. I need to act as well. After I saw what happens to children who are sold into the sex industry, I knew I couldn't just speak about it on a stage behind a microphone. I had to get involved. A few of us got together and did what we could, creating the charitable organization Stand Out International. It's not enough and it doesn't put an end to the need for action in my life. But it's a start. It's the thing I can do at the moment and it's a challenge that I'm determined to keep on facing. It's like what Pope John Paul II once said: "Faith leads us beyond ourselves." That journey of going beyond ourselves never stops, never stays the same, never grows stale. Put another way: When it comes to putting the fine words that we sing into action, the next step matters far more than the final destination.

Social justice is so hot right now. It's cool to volunteer and make a difference and it's great to be singing about the action as well as the affection. Get yourself a battered passport and a stack of overseas mission experience and you'll get some kudos at the summer festivals. But let's not allow cynicism to infect us. True, much of the church has been slow at catching on to the suffering that goes on in every corner of the world, but it doesn't mean we can't engage now. It's time we stopped looking in. It's time to look—and then get—out.

When I was in Thailand, something weird happened. Horrified by the realities of child sex exploitation, my mates and I knew we had to act. But before that, something hit us: a song. We called it "God of This City," and it just sort of arrived. I'll tell you about it later on, but here's what you need to know now: It wasn't about finding a catchy hook or quirky angle or perfect phrase; it was about seeing a need and recognizing our responsibility to fill it. Sometimes a song becomes bigger than the words and music; it becomes a channel of change. That's exactly what happened with "God of This City." It turned into a manifesto to bring about the greater things God has in mind for us—*all of us*.

Our faith, our worship, our music don't have to be fleeting. At the very core of those three things is our devotion to God, and that's something that simply has to carry on, whatever the weather. God is still the God of every city. And, yes, that includes every city that is ravaged by sexual captivity, disease, violence and bloodthirsty greed.

So I'm on a mission. Like plenty of others, I'm here to fight the powers that would have us ignore this suffering that plagues the world. I want us to look at it, to let it touch us and trouble us and keep us awake at night and bother us when we're going about our daily business. I want our knowledge of what's wrong with the world to spur us into action, to mainline adrenaline into our faith and lead us into action. I know that God is the author of making greater things erupt in this world, and that by His grace He can involve us in how He chooses to ignite transformation in the world around us. And this usually happens one small step at a time.

Some of us are too afraid to be part of the change because we are ashamed we took too long to step in. Or maybe we had some ideas that didn't work out. Or maybe we think we don't have enough to offer in serving others because we are broken in some way ourselves. Or maybe we simply do not know where to begin. Or maybe we don't care. Or maybe we think that the Church is acting best when it just makes more Christians, regardless of whether they're starving, sick or raped by tourists for $10 an hour.

Let's be honest about the world and our part in it. Let's go back to Scripture and see what it has to say about all this. Let's not be afraid of not being perfect or having it all together all the time. Let's start where we are at, build some momentum, and keep it going. Let's move forward, one foot in front of the other, to do greater things in our life, our family, our community and our city. Let's work out how we can release some of this incredible potential that is held within the Church. Let's wake up to the fact that changing the world is not up to our leaders or our elders or our richer cousins or our more radical neighbors. It's up to us. Yes, there is a time to sing and a time to weep, there are times to work and times to rest, but when it comes to problems that need fixing around us, there is never a time to stay silent.

You can join me in this mission. On these pages, we will ask some questions and search for some answers. We'll see where we can find directions and the fuel to push back the darkness and roll out the greater things that God has in store for every city and every human being.

ONE: SWEAT

"Hey there, mister, what you want? You wanna menu? I got them all for you."

"Gimme 10 dollar, I give you good time. Girl? Boy? What you want?"

"You like her and her friend? Take them both! You have good time."

Take a stroll down Walking Street in Pattaya, Thailand, and you'll hear all this. It's the center of the city's sex trade, the epicenter of the ultimate destination for sex tourists to fill whatever lusts their body craves. Located in the red-light district of the city, the street hoards clusters of go-go bars and massage parlors, all of them with a guy standing outside trying to draw you in. The sounds are innocent enough—cheap dance music played too loud on too cheap stereo systems—but it's what you see that can really bother you. The scene is a baffling montage of ladies in mini-skirts and high heels, grown men in Hollywood glam makeup wearing lingerie, and teenage boys with awkward posture and uncertainty in their eyes who parade up and down the streets beckoning sex-hungry men and women. I didn't know what to expect when I arrived in Pattaya, but it only took one trip out at night in the city for it to shock me to my core. The place is horrific.

Here you can buy anyone and do anything to him or her. Poverty and oppression collide to create a cruel playground for the depraved. You want a girl? Check out the menu. You want a boy? Name your price. Into pedophilia? Come on in. Every-one's welcome. Everything's allowed. Nobody ever says "no." Of course, this is not an isolated experience. What happens in Pat-taya is just a small-scale example of what is happening in far too many cities crisscrossing the world. Each year, millions of people are sold into modern-day slavery—we know it as human trafficking—many of whom are used for sexual exploitation.

Our eye-opening trip took place in November 2006. As a band, we had been invited by our missions pastor to head out to Pattaya with a bunch of other Christians to play at an event spon-sored by some Belfast missionaries. In an outreach called Pattaya Praise, over a span of a few days we reached out to the residents of the city by ministering messages and holding concerts that re-flected the love of God. Our mission was to shed light on the darkness that is much of Pattaya. It's a noble and worthy cause, but when you stand in the middle of the red-light district and are surrounded by the vast perversity that seeps through every pore in the city, you can't help but feel a foot tall in a land of giants.

To say we felt out of our league is an understatement. There we were, six young lads from Belfast, some of us getting our pass-ports for the first time to make the trip. We'd been told about the way things work out here, about the fact that anyone western would automatically be assumed to be there to buy sex. We were warned Pattaya was one of those places where the criminal un-derworld comes to the surface, like a volcanic hot spring channel-ing steam from way down beneath the earth's crust. Of course, not everyone in Pattaya is enmeshed or ensnared in the darkness. No doubt, plenty of good people live here and try to make it bet-ter, but to the outsider the sheer magnitude of decadence smacks you in the gut. Sexual licentiousness is to Pattaya what gambling is to Las Vegas and drug trafficking is to Colombia.

Our band was slotted to play some gigs—all made up of worship songs, really—at a couple of bars, but for the first 48 hours we didn't leave the hotel room. We were too scared. This place freaked us out, and there was no denying that fact. The fear was as heavy as the humidity. Oh, that heat. It wrapped itself around you like a cobra and wouldn't let go. It was a 24-hour sweat fest without any relief.

EACH YEAR, MILLIONS OF PEOPLE ARE SOLD INTO MODERN-DAY SLAVERY, MANY OF WHOM ARE USED FOR SEXUAL EXPLOITATION.

After our two days of being too scared to go out, we finally made it beyond the hotel. We discovered that not only did the humidity leech the life out of you, but also the smog and smoke from the tuk-tuks choked what was left of the good stuff out of the air.

There was one bright spot: the smiles. They got us every time. Women, girls, boys . . . all of them so friendly. But we only made the mistake of smiling back and starting up a conversation once. A few seconds of that was all it took for them to thrust their menus of sexual services into our hands. When we explained that we didn't want what they were selling, the pressure increased. Pretty soon it got messy, with the girls exasperated that we didn't want them and us embarrassed at the thought of a pimp coming over to accuse us of wasting time. So much for Christians making a difference.

A day or so later and we were in a bar on Walking Street, Pattaya's Champs d'Elysees; its Fifth Avenue and Las Ramblas. It was the place that the tourists flocked to in order to have a good look and stare, but it had none of the class or glitz or fun of those other destinations. This was a place where people were bought and sold, re-used, re-abused and thrown back to the trash. It was as dark a place as any I'd ever seen, and as I walked down the street early on I kept my eyes to the ground. I'm not even sure if that was out of choice. Could I even have lifted them if I had wanted to?

We'd been given a two-hour warm-up slot at the Climax Bar, a venue that doubled as a brothel. The bar was the sort of place you'd go to if you wanted to pretend that you weren't just another sex tourist. There you could order a drink, have a conversation with a girl, and then go off to your hotel to have sex. Of course you ended up paying for it, but this place tried to make it into something more like a game. This place tried to make it all seem "normal," but it was just as dirty as the rest of the city.

While we were setting up, the girls in the bar kept away from us. There were a few drinkers in there too, but it wasn't until we started playing that they showed any interest. Not that we were particularly good; all we could play were our standard worship tracks, and we only had an hour's worth of those. Still, "Blessed Be Your Name" went down particularly well with the dancers, and one obese German tourist, sandwiched by two beautiful Thai girls, regularly shouted out that we were the best band he'd ever heard.

Then something happened. The heat was oppressive and the bar owner hated putting on the air conditioning, as he thought it might make people drink less. There was sweat all over my hands, my fingertips slipping on my guitar and my eyes blurring and blinking. I was looking out but not able to see all that much. That didn't matter, though, since I felt as if I could really *see* something. It was like peeking behind a stage curtain, although the lights were too low to truly make out what was going on. But something was happening. I knew it.

It was about these girls and this bar and these men that were here to pay for sex and the fact that this was a scene being repeated across the city and across the world. It was never meant to be this way, and it did not have to stay like this. There were greater things still to come in this city.

DARKNESS SURROUNDING

But think about this: Aren't we all in the business of needing greater things? In our lives, for one? We may not be living in a sex-trade city, but we're not so far from Pattaya ourselves. We might be thousands of miles away from Asia, but we don't have to look far to see people caught up as slaves, living a life that's a million miles away from the greater things that God intended. In the western world, we are bound by the chains of consumerism. We are at the mercy of the Joneses. We sacrifice a life of spiritual and inner abundance just so we can keep up and have what our neighbor has.

Then there's the rest of the world. We don't have to look to Pattaya for the shadow of the darkness. The camps of central Africa where the refugees greet the morning sun with the suffocating tears of grief are not the only home to death and decay. Almost half the world—more than 3 billion people—lives on less than $2.50 a day.[1] There are 33.4 million people living with AIDS.[2] More than 1 billion people across the world are hungry.[3]

It's not just in the papers that we read of pain and sorrow that take our breath away. We see it in the lives of people around us, maybe even in our own life. There is darkness and suffering in the microcosms and macrocosms of this world. It is real. It inhales freedom, breathes out death, and claims lives. It enslaves, tortures and dehumanizes God's children. It chokes, bleeds and exhausts hope. It overwhelms, it traps, it kills.

One thing is for sure: We are not living the way God intended us to live. Instead of living a life rooted in peace, charity, compassion and contentment, we live with loss.

We have lost love.

We have lost hope.

We have lost faith.

We have lost mothers and fathers.

We have lost children.

We have lost partners.

We have lost work.

We have lost health.

We have lost trust.

We have lost security.

We have lost the dream of how it was all supposed to be.

We have lost what we never knew we had.

Does this mean there is nothing we can do? Are we meant now to just roll over, nurse our wounds, and leave the business of transformation to someone else? Do we just give up and let the world move forward with its own demise?

No.

We keep believing and keep praying and keep asking God to show us greater things that He can do in our lives and for the world. He is a light to the darkness everywhere—in Pattaya, in China, in your neighborhood, and in my life.

Be encouraged. Wherever there is darkness, whether in a city or a home, there can also be light.

THE LIGHT

Back at the Climax Bar, with the heat melting on my forehead and our stage presence competing with drunken men and their flirtatious lady friends, something happened. Someone was playing a riff that looped and repeated, building up to some nearby crescendo, and I started singing out.

"Greater things are yet to come. Greater things are still to be done in this city."

I couldn't help but think about the darkness of Pattaya. Was this it? Was this all Pattaya could ever be? Was this darkness fixed and unbreakable? Was there really no light in it? And these people, these slaves—was there no chance of hope for them? Was there no peace they could reach for? No change? No rescue? Were there no greater things yet to come for them?

From my heart, I kept on singing prophetic words over that city and any other city, place or person where darkness took up residence. Words of hope were all I could get out. At some point we stopped. I don't know how long we'd been in the riff or for how long we'd been on that little stage, but as I resurfaced I saw them again—the German, the women in prostitution, the shadowy men beside the bar. Some were looking back at us, others were carrying on as if it was every night of the week they had a worship band from Belfast come in and sing prophetically over them.

BE ENCOURAGED. WHEREVER THERE IS DARKNESS, WHETHER IN A CITY OR A HOME, THERE CAN ALSO BE LIGHT.

We left, knowing that something had happened, but unsure exactly what. However, there was one thing of which I was certain: Though Pattaya was a place given over to the evils of abuse and injustice, light could shine through. God could take up space in that city and crown it with beauty and glory and joy.

LOOKING IN

God is in the business of transformation, but before He can transform the world, He has to start with us. Ours is a society fuelled by consumerism. We've gone shopping for a god and come back with a god of shopping. We're full of the ideas of freedom, liberty and personal choice, and yet just one trip to buy a pair of jeans can entangle us in a web of injustice and oppression. We might think we're getting a bargain, but it's only because some poor kid has been working hunched over a sewing machine for 13 hours a day, no bathroom breaks or water, and making less than a couple of dollars in return.

We're consuming resources at a rate that is making the planet groan. Our wealth doesn't cause us to blink or pause. When was the last time you considered how much water you use? In Europe, we use an average of 50 gallons of water per day—in the United States it's closer to 100—while in the developing world that figure is more like 3 gallons.[4] Every minute of every day, three children under the age of five die because their water is unclean and they have no access to a decent toilet.[5]

While Americans make up less than 5 percent of the world's population, they consume 26 percent of the world's energy.[6] Add Canada into that equation, and both countries take up 50 percent of energy consumption.

The colossal amount of energy used in picking, packing, freezing, shipping, shopping, storing and cooking is just one of the reasons why we in the United Kingdom consume at such a rate that, if the rest of the world were to do the same, by 2050 we would need a whole 8 other extra planets to provide enough resources.

We're hyper-connected, mobile and free to live, work and love where we want, yet right now the International Labor Organization (ILO) estimates there are 12.3 million people for whom freedom is just a sick joke.[7] They're the new slaves, forced to work; adults and children forced to fight, forced to have sex, forced to the point when their lives expire. The U.S. Department of State reports that 600,000 to 800,000 individuals are trafficked across international borders each year.[8] These people are taken against their will to become slaves within the sex trade, in sweatshops, farms or homes.

Some of us know of these realities but are more comfortable viewing them from a safe distance. To others, this is something new, and they would prefer to remain blissfully ignorant, thank you very much. Either way, it is clear that many of us have created a comfortable, inward-looking existence because it's easier or cleaner or less work that way.

But even as we slumber and the world suffers, God says, "No. Greater things I have in store for the cities of the world that beg for mercy. There is light, there is peace, there is hope beyond the tears, the pain and the lack."

CREATED TO REACH

Make no mistake: Within each of us is the potential to hear the still, small voice that points us toward the light. We might feel powerless, we might feel weak, we might even doubt whether any of this is our responsibility anyway, but we cannot deny that God has placed in each of us the potential to change the world around us.

I've known what it's like to live in a comfort zone with my arms stuck at my side. I've known what it's like to feel crushed by the horror of dread coming into reality. I've known the temptation to put everything on hold and retreat. Like a hot air balloon sinking fast, I've felt as though I have wanted to ditch everything, to move to safety, to abandon all the big plans and bold hopes. I've wanted to make life small, because it's just easier that way.

But God has not called us to be safe or comfortable. He has called us to look around at the darkness and find a way to shine the spotlight of His mercy, grace, restoration and transformation. This book won't answer all of your questions about suffering or give you a blueprint of what God wants you to do about it, but it may be another small jigsaw piece that slots into your puzzle of faith. It might complete a chapter in your life. At the very least, I pray it gives you the determination to reach out. Somehow. In some way.

WHY BOTHER?

Before we continue, let me address some questions you may be chewing on.

Isn't justice best left to God?

Why do we feel that we need to help those with less?

Aren't we supposed to make disciples, not become social workers?

Isn't the message of salvation more important than some foil-packed emergency meal?

Since when is it our responsibility to save the world?

In other words, why bother?

God never intended us to keep silent, to close our eyes, to cross the road and pretend we haven't seen something that makes our stomach turn or our hearts break. Speaking and reaching out is what we were created to do. The Bible is full of daring leaders who knew how important it was to help those who needed it. Read what Job wrote. Do you think his taking an interest in the case of the poor, the orphan or the homeless had anything to do with God calling him a righteous man?

"I rescued the poor who cried for help, and the fatherless who had none to assist him . . . I was eyes to the blind and feet to the lame. I was a father to the needy; I took up the case of the stranger. I broke the fangs of the wicked and snatched the victims from their teeth" (Job 29:12,15-17).

Or what about the Old Testament prophets like Amos, Isaiah or Micah? You can read through all the books they wrote in the Bible and come up with a stack of verses about reaching and speaking out. Amos, for instance, shook his fist and admonished those whose greed blinded them and who took advantage of poor people. "Hear this, you who trample the needy and do away with the poor of the land, saying, 'When will the New Moon be over that we may sell grain, and the Sabbath be ended that we may market wheat?'—skimping the measure, boosting the price and cheating with dishonest scales, buying the poor with silver and the needy for a pair of sandals, selling even the sweepings with the wheat" (Amos 8:4-6).

Amos was laying into the corrupt businessmen of the day. These guys were on the wrong side of God's favor because of their shady dealings. To name a few offenses, they couldn't wait to get the trade-free Sabbath and Festival days over and done with so that they could get back to business. They grossly inflated their prices and even messed with their measuring scales to cheat others into giving them a bigger profit.

The writer of Proverbs was on the money when he wrote that "a poor man's field may produce abundant food, but injustice sweeps it away" (Prov. 13:23). Jesus was right when He said that "the worker deserves his wages" (Luke 10:7). We don't know what Jesus' spending habits were like, but we do know how He taught us to treat people through His example. Is there anything that would make us think that He might have screwed people for every shekel He could get? Is there any evidence to suggest that His lifestyle and character weren't perfectly aligned? Did He not live out His words, "Greater love has no one than this, that he lay down his life for his friends" (John 15:13)? And remember what He said right before: "My command is this: Love each other as I have loved you" (John 15:12).

Could it be any clearer? From the prophets of old to the Savior of today, our mission is simple: to reach out, speak up and express our love for God and others through the way we talk, shop, act, live, vote, argue and engage. We were made to reflect God's glory—the very same God who spoke our world into existence out of the darkness; the very same God who revealed Himself through His Son; the very same God whose Spirit still speaks to us today.

How could we ever believe that silence or doing nothing was an option?

MY CONFESSION

I want to confess something. Right up to the point when the Lord inspired me with this song on the Climax Bar stage, I did not really believe any of this. I don't know why I went to Pattaya, but I know it wasn't to break the chains of injustice. Maybe I was locked into an insular way of being—seeing the world through the eyes of the Church, rather than the other way around. Maybe I thought we were there to lead worship and that the battle was one that needed to be carried out in the spiritual, rather than the physical, realm.

How wrong I was.

Sometimes you have to be shaken at your core before you realize your responsibility to reach out and love others; before you realize you have to do more than sing on a stage an arm's length away from others.

SOMETIMES YOU HAVE TO BE SHAKEN AT YOUR CORE BEFORE YOU REALIZE YOUR RESPONSIBILITY TO REACH OUT AND LOVE OTHERS.

There's a story I read about a man named Harry. He's a pastor in a small village somewhere down below the equator—Malawi, I think—who owned five cows. And that was a pretty good thing. Those animals were his business, his pension, his health care plan and his savings, all rolled into one. If anything ever went wrong, he knew that he'd be able to sell one of the beasts and that the money would be enough to cover any unforeseen emergency.

Being a pastor in a small village didn't mean that Harry got a house, a salary or a shiny new 4x4 every other year. It just meant that he led, taught, supported, soothed, prayed and devoted his life to the rest of the village as well as his own family. He was a remarkable man.

So, Harry, his wife and his five kids relied on their cattle. But one day there were only four. No warning signs, no illness, no "I'm off to find a better life" note scratched in the dirt. Just one dead cow lying on the ground. It was a big deal.

A while later, the big deal became even bigger: another cow was found dead. This time there were signs: a wound in the animal's side, a flow of blood marking the exit of life from this innocent animal. It was a deliberate attack. Now Harry was left with just three cows.

This crisis was the source of every conversation throughout the village. The people were shocked. Harry knew all eyes were fixed on him. How would he react? Would he get mad? Seek revenge? Spew his anger at God?

No. Instead, Harry forgave. He was tempted not to, of course, but he forgave the killer of his cows. The people looked on in surprise, and even shock. What kind of man would quickly forgive someone who stole and murdered an innocent family's livelihood? Harry's loss became others' gain, as villagers were intrigued by his reaction and took a fresh interest in his faith.

There's a point to this story, and it's not about cows or poverty. Harry's actions challenged a mindset that was preventing his village from moving ahead in a number of ways. They were materially poorer because of their refusal to help each other, and their sense of community was also held back, stunted and starved. It was as if they had a set of chains around their wrists and ankles, holding them back, breaking their skin. Harry explained, "In the village there has been a belief that if I am lacking, then I cannot assist anyone. But we told people that in the midst of lacking there is something that I can assist my friend with."

The people in the village were so moved by Harry's mercy that this message of hope and help finally took hold. They began to care for their own, even though they did not have much in their own pockets. The church pooled what little resources they had and rebuilt the home of an old blind man in the village. They also bought a school uniform for a poor girl and repaired the roof of an old lady. Their eyes have been opened, their hearts changed, and life in the village has improved overall. There has been an obvious transformation.

All it took was a couple of dead cows and a faithful man who refused to give in to fear and anger.

WHAT NEXT?

Since having my physical and spiritual eyes opened in Pattaya, to this day I've been on a journey. A few years ago, if I'd been in Harry's shoes, I would have fought for revenge. Forgiveness would only have crossed my mind once I'd extracted some payback. But something happened in that special Thai city that started a change in me. It's made me realize that what I believe and how I live are meant to be intertwined. It's made me hungry to write songs with actions—not the cute ones we teach the kids in Sunday School, but the ones we absorb into our lives and put into glorious flesh and blood. It's made me look up, look out, and look for the ways in which some of this potential I have can be put to better use than making me more comfortable.

So how do we react to the suffering that permeates countless cities all over the world? How do those of us who say we believe in God—who try to listen for what He says and then follow whatever instructions we decipher, no matter how faint the whisper or how frequent our failings—respond to these troubling realities? What do we do with the knowledge that we share the planet with such suffering?

Do we take this fight on as our own, or do we retreat into our churches to celebrate and sing?

Do we rise up and wrestle with the injustice, or do we close our ears, eyes and hearts?

Do we speak out, or do we hope that a mumbled prayer will do?

Do we go, or do we freeze?

This book is a part of the journey of you answering those questions. It's not a map to take you to the final destination; it's a compass to better position yourself where you need to be heading. I have no doubt that God will lead you exactly where He sees you fitting in this grand equation. Just open up to possibilities, trust Him, and watch with bated breath as God slowly unravels greater things.

TWO: US?

Take a look at three scenarios where the message of Jesus has been mangled to suit agendas, opinions or fears.

There was a church that was doing well. It was serving the needs of an increasing number of people, and there was a buzz about the services. Then the gas station across the road got some new owners. They were Muslim. The church, which had never really done a lot in the community itself, decided that this was the time to stand up and speak out. They arranged for placards and signs to be placed outside their building, warning all congregation members and passers-by to join in a boycott of the Muslim-owned gas station.

There was a pastor at a growing church. He was an intelligent guy and an electric speaker. One night the church was even more packed than usual, and the pastor was up on stage introducing a friend of his who had recently been in the news for something big. Holding this guy's hand, the pastor found a comedic groove that had the church chuckling. "Thankfully, this guy's not one of those new gay clergy," he chimed. "I wouldn't be holding his hand if he was." Cue big laughter from many and looks of shame and embarrassment for a few.

At a conference in front of thousands of people, a new director of a recently relaunched charity was invited up to share the platform with the host. He was introduced and given a decent reception. Then came the question—the opportunity for the director to secure himself a whole new batch of recruits: "In your opinion, what is it that the Church needs most right now?" The answer? "More people like me."

None of these stories show these people at their best. They're all capable of so much more, but these episodes would leave most people shaking their heads in embarrassment. We are supposed to be living examples of God, but sometimes we get the whole example part wrong. We put up our agenda instead of His, because we think we need to protect God, the Church or ourselves. And when we calculate our life steps our own way, it can make loving or serving or giving or sacrificing feel more foreign than anything.

WE ARE SUPPOSED TO BE LIVING EXAMPLES OF GOD, BUT SOMETIMES WE GET THE WHOLE EXAMPLE PART WRONG.

When we carve out our own grooves in this journey of life, we can do some serious damage to people. Sometimes our mistakes are colossal; sometimes they are small. Sometimes we leave people embittered and angry; at other times our words and actions just leave a stale taste in their mouth. While we might do it in a variety of ways, the roots remain the same: we substitute our plans for God's. We take out our own compass, our own maps, our own boots and proclaim that they must all be leading in the direction God ordains.

This, of course, is nothing new. We've been good at moving the goalposts closer to ourselves for . . . well, forever. Snaking through the history of Christianity are cases of believers willing to twist their beliefs around to suit whatever outcome they wish, even if that meant bullying, fighting and killing. Just look at what a handful of the popes did a few centuries ago:

- Pope Alexander VI was a mistress-bedding, murdering, power-grabbing despot.

- Pope Sixtus IV, during the time of the Spanish Inquisition, introduced the torture of waterboarding to the work of the Church in a misguided attempt to ensure that new Christian converts had the proper theological understanding.

- Pope Leo X financed his ambitious building program by selling a certificate that absolved you of all sin—past, present and future—if the price was right.

- Pope Stephen VI dug up the corpse of his predecessor and adversary, Formosus. He put the rotting corpse on trial and attempted to have public opinion turned against the memory of the man. He failed.

But this is no anti-Catholic trip. The Protestant Church has given us it's own charlatans, conmen, liars, cheats, embezzlers, fraudsters and imperfect heroes.

- Queen Elizabeth had Catholics murdered for not converting to Protestantism.

- Calvin approved the burning of heretics in Geneva, Switzerland.

- Martin Luther penned anti-Semitic diatribes and recommended that Christians destroy Jewish synagogues and homes.

- Numerous contemporary evangelists and pastors have been ensnared in various sex and money scandals.

We've become quite good at swinging the message of the cross around to make us rich, isolated, uncaring and superior to the army of poor sinners outside our doors.

NOT US

The thing is, we are not the ones in control. We don't have the power. We are not the driver behind the wheel of life. God is. The story of life is not about us. It's about God.

Day in and day out, we get confused about the role we have. We forget that we are here to follow, to serve, to obey and to experience the glorious freedom found in doing all these things for God. We fail miserably when we put ourselves at the heart of the action and plot our lives according to whatever North our appetites happen to select.

Blaise Pascal, the French mathematician and philosopher, got it right when he wrote, "God made man in his own image and man returned the compliment." How many of us have made God into a human version of ourselves? How many of us play dress-up in the robes of the divine? That's what the religious leaders I talked about earlier did. Somehow, the result is not quite as cute as it sounds.

Think about it this way. Phrases such as "I feel the Lord telling me to . . ." or "I sense that the Lord is calling me to . . ." are hardly ever followed by words such as ". . . put my personal goals aside and follow Him wherever that may be" or ". . . live alongside the poor" or ". . . downsize and give up my possessions to the needy."

More often, these phrases are twinned with these kinds of follow-ups: ". . . follow the dream of becoming an internationally recognized worship leader" or ". . . move up the property ladder" or ". . . start a new business."

Okay, so these might be cheap examples, but you get the point. We're well practiced at putting ourselves at the heart of how we feel life should be designed for us. Like Blaise Pascal said, we're making God in our own image. Frankly, I don't think He's all that impressed.

I remember hearing about a trip that Jackie Pullinger made back to the United Kingdom a few years ago. If you don't know her, here's a little bio: wealthy, well-educated London girl abandons promising musical career to follow a hunch that God might want her to travel east. She ended up among the drugs and violence and crime and abuse of Hong Kong's Walled City. For decades, she devoted herself to the addicts and the ones that society would rather forget. There was no glamour, only hard work and continual sacrifice, and God was all over it.

When Jackie came back, she started talking to people about some new things in the charismatic movement that she heard had been going on in the Church. It was the time of the Toronto Blessing—a period in the 1990s when people flooded from around the world to a small church in Canada that was full of Christians soaking up the Holy Spirit. Jackie had heard all about it and had a unique perspective on the events. "We heard that there were Christians jumping on airplanes to fly to the place where the laughter was," she said. "We thought it was strange. Why would people do that? Why would Christians spend their time and money chasing after laughter when there is so much sorrow and pain and suffering in this world? But we told each other that it would only be a matter of time before people started to get onto the planes to come to the places where the crying was. We waited. But you never came."

I don't believe God is behind the motives of creating inclusive Christian churches, or the people who tell us to stay within the church, who say nothing about poverty, injustice, slavery or oppression, who talk about what's wrong with everyone outside the building, who preach hatred and division, and who stay silent on hope. These are people and organizations who twist a religion to suit their fancy.

HIDING

There have been so many times that I've been guilty of doing my own thing instead of surrendering my architectural plans to God. I did this by hiding. If I turn my mind back to the way I was when I was growing up, I can't help but feel embarrassed. I used to be the kind of kid who thought going to church was about pleasing people—not just to make them happy, but also to get some satisfaction from their approval. I don't think God ever came into my faith or, let's call it what it really was, church-going life. I just went because it got my parents off my back. I went because they wanted me to, so perhaps I didn't want to let them down.

But the truth was that I was letting them down. Colossally. I was a violent, drunken, drugged, criminal, thuggish, petty, bitter and angry young man who used church attendance as an innocent mask to hide behind. I was wrong. There was no hiding.

God was not impressed with my fake performance. When my parents found out the truth about my life, they weren't particularly pleased either. Nothing good came out of my hypocrisy. I don't even think I made any more friends. All I know for sure is that in trying to make myself the star of my own life, I messed up. I got nowhere in my spiritual life and lived a bland, unmeaningful existence.

EVERYTHING

Let me make one thing clear: I believe God is the beginning and end of existence. He is our all. He is everything. Without Him, we are nothing. To me, that is an absolute truth, although I know we live in an era where relativism is more attractive, where we are all supposed to be allowed to believe whatever it is we want. *My truth is just my truth*, so we are told. *Yours will be your own. Nothing is concrete. We are all embers from the same fire. There is one mountain of faith, with many ways up.*

Rubbish.

I'll admit that there are some things that are gray—much of life, in fact, is far less of an either/or affair than we might think. But there are some things that are true and some that are not true, some things that are right and some things that are wrong, some things that define us and some that separate us.

Like the fact that our God is above all things and is our everything. There are imitations and fake make-overs, but there really is no one like our God. No man, woman, child or shiny new product that guarantees smooth lines and perfect curves can ever come close. Nothing can ever compare to the glory, the beauty, the majesty, the power, the kindness, the grace and the forgiveness of our God. Beyond our comprehension, above our best attempts at goodness, beneath our claims at owning the land we stand on, we find God. The first, the last, the beginning and the end, the death-conquering, life-giving source of all that was, that is, and is to come.

That's our God.

Pretty impressive, huh?

Honestly, if you had the chance of serving, loving and being loved and shaped by such a God, would you ever settle for anything less? Would you even contemplate looking elsewhere? Of course not. And yet that's precisely what we do. Time and time again.

CHOICE

Now, how can we expect God to reign over our cities and bring about restoration and transformation in this world if we won't even let Him reign over our lives? It's simple. It won't happen.

It comes down to making a simple decision: Do we give God control, or do we orchestrate our own life and its paths? This is a natural tension that has been documented throughout the ages—the choice between something good and eternal or something that only provides temporary satisfaction.

To eat the apple or not eat the apple was not a question of two happy campers fancying a wee snack; it was a deeper matter. It had to do with whether or not Adam and Eve would follow their own desires or God's instructions. Biblical history shows us that God has a tendency for trying desperately to make us see how much better life is if we choose Him.

HOW CAN WE EXPECT GOD TO REIGN OVER OUR CITIES AND BRING ABOUT RESTORATION IF WE WON'T EVEN LET HIM REIGN OVER OUR LIVES?

God did not lead the Israelites on a 40-year journey through the wilderness because He'd lost the map; He did it to teach them the importance of putting their whole trust in Him, of their choosing to follow Him as their one true God. This same God did not yell at Amos, "Away with the noise of your songs!" because He'd gone off harps and lyres for the time being and fancied something a little more punky. God was raging against the injustice of greed and corruption at that time, the fruit of a mind that says I matter more than you do, my way or the highway.

Scripture reveals the benefits of doing life the right way, God's way. Look at the Early Church. Why do you think they grew so fast? Was it because the apostles had a good strategy? Had they cracked the code and worked out the ultimate church-planting model? Had they become the experts? Not quite. They grew because, as Luke explains in Acts 2, they lived precisely the kind of God-and-others-focused lives the Gospels teach:

> They devoted themselves to the apostles' teaching and to the fellowship, to the breaking of bread and to prayer. Everyone was filled with awe, and many wonders and miraculous signs were done by the apostles. All the believers were together and had everything in common. Selling their possessions and goods, they gave to anyone as he had need. Every day they continued to meet together in the temple courts. They broke bread in their homes and ate together with glad and sincere hearts, praising God and enjoying the favor of all the people. And the Lord added to their number daily those who were being saved (Acts 2:42-47).

Think about when Jesus hung on the cross. Could there be a clearer image of the importance, the difficulty and the incredible power that is found within a life devoted to obeying God? Don't think He didn't have a choice. While He was praying in the garden, He had asked God if maybe, just maybe, there was another way out of this. But while that trepidation rocked His soul momentarily, He knew His ultimate choice was to follow God's plan.

SHIFT

Why does this tension exist? Why is the decision to drop our desires, pick up our cross, and follow God so hard sometimes? Perhaps it's just human nature. Perhaps it's precisely because we were designed to follow God but have been given free will that we have this tendency to so elevate our own wills and appetites. God's shoes are big ones to fill, after all.

But perhaps some of us put ourselves on the throne of our own kingdoms not because we're being deliberately disobedient, but because there seems to be an absence of any other voice leading us on. Learning to obey God is one thing, but some of us are struggling to even hear Him to begin with. Our lives are so bent around the habit of following our own lead that we can get easily confused and become deaf to any voice other than our own. How do we make a shift from listening to our inner guidance and hearing and listening to God's?

Reading Psalm 34 might help illustrate this a little. King David wrote this song after a weird encounter with his enemy King Abimilech. Instead of trusting in God to save him from the adversary, David pretended to be insane to save his own skin. Later he wrote, "I sought the LORD, and he answered me; he delivered me from all my fears" (Ps. 34:4).

David finally gets things in the right order: searching, hearing and then getting yanked out of the situation he needs yanking out of. I think that's not such a bad system to follow, and

I'm pretty sure that David is not the only celebrated God-chaser who has done things that way.

Listen. Hear. Accept God's intervention.

We can be tempted to do things the other way round—to look for the fix in any given situation and then try to work out what God might be saying. Only after that comes the serious prayer time. It might only be a subtle shift, but it's all part of this DNA that strives to put us back in control, to have us take charge of our affairs and turn God into some kind of cartoon genie in a cartoon bottle.

It's time to shift out of the driver's seat and surrender the steering wheel to God. Only then can we be ready for God to do some serious business in changing the world, healing souls, feeding the hungry, clothing the naked, restoring the sick and bringing abundance in a land that lacks.

THE ME-FIRST CULTURE

Saying yes to God means saying no to the messages in our culture that tell us we're supposed to take control of our own lives; that we're meant to be in charge. Ads have been telling us for years that we're worth it—and that the "it" in question can cover anything from shampoo to massive debt, overconsumption to easy abortion. We might be slowly waking up to the fact that there are consequences to the way that we treat the planet, but we're still a million miles away from dismantling the me-first culture.

But people are trying. Listen carefully enough, read widely enough, and you can see signs of rebellion in the ranks. I read an article in *The Times Online* that introduced a book, *A Good*

Childhood: Searching for Values in a Competitive Age, written by Dr. Rowan Williams. In this book, Dr. Williams reports his conclusions of a two-year study of modern childhood. Specifically, he exposes the negative effects on children who come from broken homes. The article opened:

> Children's lives are being blighted by "obsessive" testing, relentless advertising and a long-hours culture that contributes to family breakdown, the Archbishop of Canterbury says in a report published today. In a scathing attack on a society that he says is organized around the needs and desires of adults, Dr Rowan Williams argues that people must change their ways if Britain is to become a better place for children to grow up in.[1]

"A society . . . organized around the needs and desires of adults"—it's the same gene we've been looking at in this chapter, the me-first/God-last approach to life. It's become so embedded in our society and has sunk so deep into the earth around our roots that our children are now paying the price. Dr. Williams's conclusions suggest that there are signs that this me-first world doesn't work quite as well as we hoped it might. Think about what a me-focused attitude has brought us in our families: long hours at work, crazy scheduling of childcare and pre-/after-school clubs, weekends where each partner carves out their allotted "me-time," trips to play-facilities where the two kids will happily wander off and be amused while dad takes a break.

Life like this is hard. Having it all—the career, the marriage, the body, the wardrobe, the bank balance, the social life, the perfect family unit—is fool's gold. And because we're fully signed up to the consumerist mindset, we believe that like personal trainers and cookery courses, our parenting can be taken care of if we buy the right resources. Cram the week with after-school activities, bloat the weekends with sports, take holidays in places where the kids will have people to look after them, and you've succeeded in being a good parent.

In all of this, we've mastered the art of living a fast pace. Just look how frantic we are in our search for the new thing that will reinvent, redefine, readjust or make our lives just right. This pace has accelerated so much that it has become almost impossible to decipher where we're at anymore. We may think that there are few defining moments going on around us, but we'd be wrong. The truth is that we're surrounded by white noise and static as values, trends, ideals and powers shift with each rising sun.

In the same way that our families are suffering and our identities are becoming increasingly egocentric, our churches are becoming so insular—focusing on building projects, hiring the hot new worship leader, or enlarging the youth group—that it's easy to miss God. So easy, in fact, that sometimes we can't hear Him at all.

For some reason, I'm now remembering the scene from the movie *Fight Club* where the main character, Tyler (played by Brad Pitt), is burning the narrator's (Ed Norton) hand with lye.

> **Tyler Durden:** Shut up! Our fathers were our models for God. If our fathers bailed, what does that tell you about God?

Narrator: No, no, I . . . don't . . .

Tyler Durden: Listen to me! You have to consider the possibility that God does not like you. He never wanted you. In all probability, He hates you. This is not the worst thing that can happen.

Narrator: It isn't?

Tyler Durden: We don't need him!

It's clumsy, but it makes a point. When all we have is what we can see, when our aspirations are printed on magazine covers or in a million dancing pixels, when we make God in our own image, then there really is no need for God at all. And when life begins and ends with us, when all that matters is all that we can control, then we're left utterly responsible for our own success.

That's a horrible place to be in. It makes life small, as Eugene Peterson points out: "The secularized mind is terrorized by mysteries. Thus it makes lists, labels people, assigns roles, and solves problems. But a solved life is a reduced life. These tightly buttoned up people never take great faith risks or make convincing love talk. They deny or ignore the mysteries and diminish human existence to what can be managed, controlled and fixed. We live in a cult of experts who explain and solve. The vast technological apparatus around us gives the impression that there is a tool for everything if only we can afford it."[2]

WHAT HAPPENS WHEN YOU FOLLOW

Some see the decision to follow God as a sign of weakness. Some say it shows a failure to make something of ourselves. Some say it means giving up personal freedom. I can see why people would think that, but they've missed the point entirely. Putting God in control, following the great commandment to love Him and others, makes for the most liberated life ever.

Some of you might remember the story of the Good Samaritan you heard about in Sunday School or in church (see Luke 10:25-37). A Jewish man was beaten to a bloody pulp and left for dead on the side of the road. A total of three people passed this man. One was a priest, the second a Temple assistant; both walked by without stopping to help. The third, a Samaritan who was hated solely because of his ethnicity, helped this man, nursed him and carried him to an inn to rest.

The Jewish leaders come out of this story looking pretty bad. But their lack of inaction is not entirely selfish. You have to understand the backdrop of the laws of that time. They were doing what was right according to the moral code—keeping away from the uncleanliness of the beaten and bloodied man— but it was too narrow a definition of "the right thing" for Jesus. While these religious leaders were following the law, they never considered the merits of compassion and mercy, the very things that propel us beyond ritual and religion and the safety of our legalism.

This is what following God does. It makes us leap over our walls of comfort and rules into a space where we can act out the character of God in life-changing ways. This is how the world can change. This is how our cities can change. This is how our lives can change. All of this can happen when we focus on the bigger picture of living out the gospel of Jesus instead of boxing ourselves into a religion we contort to satisfy our comfort level.

Jesus was talking about this very thing when, in His last sermon, He accused the religious leaders of the day of being like "whitewashed tombs, which look beautiful on the outside but on the inside are full of dead men's bones and everything unclean" (Matt. 23:27). Back in the day, whitewashing a tomb was a good thing to do. By painting them, the owner was making sure that passers-by could spot the graves and avoid touching them, thus keeping themselves free from becoming unclean. In other words, those head honchos were doing everything right on the outside, but their spiritual life on the inside was rotten.

FOLLOWING GOD MAKES US LEAP OVER OUR WALLS OF COMFORT INTO A SPACE WHERE WE CAN ACT OUT THE CHARACTER OF GOD IN LIFE-CHANGING WAYS.

Today, Jesus reminds us that following Him and serving God is not a matter of getting the rules right. Those rules were never given to be the final destination of our faith. They were given to show us the way to God and to remind us of the way that God would have us live. Those ancient laws were meant to be interpreted through the lens of the greatest commandment delivered by Jesus in Matthew 22:37, Mark 12:30 and Luke 10:27: to love God with all our heart, soul and mind. This was something that Moses knew as well and taught the Israelites (see Deut. 6:5; Lev. 19:18).

Following God is about compassion, mercy, service and devotion. It's about saying no to our own desires, however pure we
may think they are, and devoting our lives to loving God and
others and aligning our desires with His. If we can allow this
foundational truth to shape and direct our lives, then we automatically line up for a bolder, brighter, better life. The very sort
that God intended.

I truly believe that there is no one like our God and that He
has the power to initiate life-changing actions. If we want a part
of that ride, we have to trust and serve Him first. We have to lay
down our tasks lists and agendas. We have to submit to His
lordship and follow His way. That's the genesis of bettering the
conditions of this world.

THREE: HISTORY

God is in the transformation business. Make no mistake about it, God never tires of putting things right and building His kingdom. And to be a part of that outreach, we need to jump on His bandwagon. We have to propel ourselves into action, getting off the sidelines and into the game where we belong. Of course, nothing happens overnight, but we all have to start somewhere. For me, it started with conversion.

MY CHANGE

I've told you how I was a fake when I was at church. When I wasn't turning up for Sunday services wearing my suit—or, in fact, not wearing a suit, but rebelling by wearing a nice sweater and some freshly ironed trousers—I was a thug with a scarf over my face hurling bricks at the police. They'd be there with their riot vans and protective body armor, while we'd be hurling our rubbles and feeling like real men. Or we'd be drunk, laying into each other with all the force we could. Or we'd be taking drugs or getting drunk or stealing whatever nonsense we thought we could get away with—but still impress each other. I was a teenager desperately in need of change.

Fighting was a way of life in Belfast. As a matter of fact, you could set your clocks by the riots. It didn't even matter who was on the other side. Catholics were good sport, but my mates and I didn't mind taking down other Protestants. We picked a fight with anybody for whatever random reason we could come up with. All we cared about was getting the first and the last punches in.

All this changed over the period of a year. It started one summer when I'd been dragged to an outdoor summer festival organized by some local churches. I spent much of my time there drifting around the edges of the big meetings. During one of the services, I found myself watching a man dance as part of his worship. I'd grown used to the free-spirited, charismatic spirit of the crowds, and though it had interested me, I still labeled the loud and dramatic singing, dancing and praying as a revved-up version of what we used to do in our fancy clothes back at church.

But this dancing man . . . this was something different. I'd never seen this kind of passion. I was hooked. Eventually he stopped, and we had a chance to speak for a bit. He told me which church he went to—some out-of-the-way place miles from my neighborhood. Although my life stayed pretty much the same a year after that, I never forgot the name of the church he mentioned.

I spent the next summer hanging out with my mate Ding and our friend Hazel, "the Ginge." The Ginge had two things of interest to me and Ding: a car and faith. The three of us always had a great time together, no matter what we were doing.

One Sunday night, the name of the church that the dancer had slipped in our conversation popped into my head. I decided we should take a mini road trip and visit, although I wasn't sure exactly where it was. We drove down south towards the general vicinity, hoping we'd find it right off the main road. No such luck. There was no sign of the building in the town where we ended up.

Frustrated but not ready to give up, I knocked on the door of a random house along the road. A couple of Scots answered, and I went into my speech. "Hi, guys. Listen, this is totally random, but you don't happen to know where a church called 'River of Life' is, do you? I thought it was round here, but I can't find it at all."

They stared back at me in what appeared to be confusion. Maybe it had something to do with my accent. I was about to repeat my spiel a little more slowly when they piped up in excited voices.

"Weird? A little. We've just had a call from a friend giving us directions to that same church. We're house-sitting, and he thought we might want to join him."

That was it. It had to be more than mere coincidence. Something was up. God was clearly in control of stirring up the dry bones in my life. Ding, the Ginge and I followed the Scots to church, which happened to be nowhere near where I thought it was. When we arrived, instantly a woman in the congregation started prophesying in a way that sent shivers down my spine. My soul was being moved to new heights. It was like nothing I had ever experienced before.

Driving home, I was so stirred in my soul that I made the Ginge pull over. "That's it," I confessed. "I'm finished with the old life. From now on I'm a believer and I'm following God all the way." I had a conversion of direction, of spirit, of purpose. My transformation was a cocktail of all manner of things— divine intervention, the support of friends, my curiosity, and waking up to the fact that a life of selfishness and hatred simply wasn't all it was cracked up to be.

THE EARLY CHURCH

Ever since I got on track with God, I've been fascinated with many of the early Christians who understood the importance of transformation, of change, of doing things different for a purpose. These Christians made changes on all levels—large and small.

For instance, in the first century, the Church started off following the Jewish tradition of meeting on a Saturday, but down the road their main gatherings changed to take place on a Sunday. It makes sense when you see why. The Jewish people went to Temple on Saturday, the last day of the week, thus following the tradition of the Genesis story, with God resting at the end of a busy work-filled week.

While this way of emphasizing God's ownership of creation made sense to the Jews, the Christians wanted to highlight another element of God's character. Meeting on Sunday, at the start of the week, was a powerful symbol that showed how the Church wanted to line itself up with God's transformation of the darkness, with the very start of His creation, with the day on which Christ rose from the dead. For those early Christians, it wasn't possible to separate God's capacity to transform from their beliefs and traditions.

The Early Church wasn't into name-checking God and His power. They were involved in His work. They were a catalyst for change across the world. One way this was evident was by the sheer volume of Christians who existed. Not more than 70 years after Jesus died and was resurrected, those initial handful of believers had grown into an army of more than 1 million. Imagine that: 100 to 1,000,000 in only a couple of generations. The rate of increase continued, and within a couple of centuries Christianity was adopted by about 15 million individuals across the Roman Empire in spite of the threat of persecution by the Emperor Diocletian. A decade later, and 40 million Christians covered the planet, 1 in 4 of every living soul on the planet.

AT THE HEART OF HAVING A RELATIONSHIP WITH GOD IS THE OPPORTUNITY TO BECOME A PARTNER WITH HIM IN THE BUILDING OF HIS KINGDOM.

God has been and will always be in the business of transformation, but don't misunderstand me. It's not just about boosting the numbers. At the heart of having a relationship with God is the opportunity to become a partner with Him in the building of His kingdom. What does that mean? It means expanding greater things in every city, bringing health, healing, restoration, freedom and peace. It means giving strength to those who are weak, showing love to those who are broken, and bringing joy to those who mourn.

It means following in the footsteps of our predecessors who have done those very things.

THE GOOD DOCTOR POPE

The Church was not in a good state back in A.D. 590. In fact, it was in a very bad state. Some people in political power had been trying to pursue personal integrity and do the right thing, but many leaders of influence were corrupt, greedy and in desperate need of change.

Their moral sickness had spread throughout the Church. Standards were slipping and reputations were being marred. Many internal fights broke out because of differences of opinion in doctrine, and some priests had even got in the habit of forming violent mobs whenever they didn't get their way. Bribery was rampant; if you had the money, you could buy your way into a position of power. There seemed to be more bad than good in the Church.

Help came in the form of a man who wanted nothing to do with the job. Pope Gregory I, better known as Gregory the Great, was born into a wealthy family, but his early privilege didn't make him a stranger to troubles. Rome was a dangerous place, and during his childhood Gregory was a victim of the hostile takeover of his city on three separate occasions. Well-educated and having close connections with the Roman Church, he was appointed Prefect of the City when he was 30 years old. He didn't stay in power long, by his own choice. Gregory decided his life was better served as a monk, and he severed his ties to politics. Not only that, but he gave away his fortune and established seven monasteries with the proceeds.

Gregory only managed to find solitude and seclusion for three years, as he was then ordained by the Roman Church as one of seven deacons (*regionarii*) of Rome. A year later, he was appointed by Pope Pelagius II as an ambassador to the Imperial Court in Constantinople. For six years Gregory did the job he was sent to do, but all the time he faced the challenge of believing in a simpler way of life while being surrounded by the extravagance and excess of his political and religious colleagues.

Eventually the job came to an end, and Gregory was able to return to the lifestyle and the monastery he loved. Upon settling in his beloved roots, he had a chance encounter with some English boys being sold at a Roman slave market. They were called "Angles," which was short for Anglo-Saxons, but Gregory referred to them as angels. Deciding that God was calling him to travel north, he organized a mission trip to the angels' homeland to bring the gospel to England.

Yet again Rome had other ideas, and just three days into his journey north, Gregory had to put his plans on hold and return home. He sent Augustine in his place, and the mission was successful. Because of Gregory's initiative and far-reaching vision, a sea of converts were birthed in England, and Christianity took a major step forward in spreading its message beyond the confines of the Roman empire.

Gregory's problems were not over just yet. Italy was in crisis, as floods had ruined crops and grain stores. Death and disease settled on the city in 589, with mass graves filling up out beyond the city walls. At times Gregory wanted out—there's even a story about him making a failed escape by getting lowered down the city walls in a basket—but he devoted himself to the task that God had given him, becoming pope in 590.

For 14 years—his final ones on earth—Pope Gregory I put up with all manner of illness and pain as he struggled with his work. Yet he managed to turn things around. Once more he called the Church back to its senses, putting morality, ethics and character at the top of his list of priorities. Among other things, he questioned whether being religious or making public displays of repentance was ever really enough, and introduced policies that would protect and care for the city's many refugees.

Throughout his papacy, Gregory refused to call himself Pope but referred to himself as the "servant of the servants of the Lord." His humility, sacrifice, determination and strength brought the Church back to some of its former health. Gregory the Great was indeed that. He was a legend, and through him God was able to work to transform the lives of those who needed his help the most.

OTHER KINGDOM BUILDERS

There are other stories of individuals who have found themselves caught up in God's drive for transformation by paying attention to and doing something about the ignored and neglected ills of society. History is charged with many Christians from all walks of life who have shown us the right way to go about God's business.

I think about the days of the Christian social activists during the Victorian era. They were a fired up bunch, passionate about evangelism and social issues. Even though the Anglican church at that point had little time for the poor or the oppressed, this group took the living, breathing, live-saving, hope-restoring gospel deep into the slums and to the front benches of the Houses of Parliament. And they saw results. Incredible results.

Groups like the Salvation Army endured a whole load of abuse and lame jokes for the uniforms they wore (I guess some things never change, huh?), but their Methodist founders—William and Catherine Booth—had bigger dealings to worry about. They took the gospel to the drug addicts, women in prostitution and alcoholics, providing for them and equipping them with whatever they needed in order to thrive in life and follow Christ.

I think of men like the Irish philanthropist Thomas Barnardo. He couldn't stand the thought or the sight of so many orphaned and abandoned children, so he set up orphanages all over the United Kingdom. Because of his efforts, nearly 60,000 orphans were rescued from the streets. Lord Shaftesbury, a champion of children's rights during the Victorian era, did something similar. Exerting his political influence, he set up schools that provided kids trapped by poverty with a decent education and opportunities for a brighter future. Shaftesbury also used his power to advocate better working conditions for factory and mine workers.

William Gladstone, a four-time Prime Minister of the United Kingdom, was bothered by what he saw as the root of so many of society's problems: too much booze and sex. He implemented policies restricting the sale of alcohol and making prohibition an option in each borough. Gladstone also took it upon himself to rescue women in prostitution from a life of shame and abuse.

Everywhere you looked, there were countless Christians using their potential to usher in transformation. George and Richard Cadbury—the guys who made a fortune selling chocolate—redefined what it meant to be a good employer. Not only did they pay a fair wage and offer decent conditions, but these socially aware Quakers also built houses, schools, hospitals, parks and leisure facilities for their workers.

Yet you can't beat the story of William Wilberforce. It was back on March 25, 1807, that the British Parliament passed the Slave Trade Act, abolishing slavery throughout what, at that time, was a massive British Empire. Wilberforce was one of the leaders who catapulted this cause. He was joined by Olaudah Equiano, a former slave turned popular author and anti-slavery campaigner, who shared his first-hand account of what life was like for slaves.

These men, and other men and women like them, allowed their faith and politics to combine and produce a thoroughly righteous outcome all over the world.

WHAT HAVE WE DONE?

These are good stories. I like them—they leave me feeling encouraged and inspired and proud of the work that my fellow believers have accomplished with God's grace.

But I'll be honest: these stories scare me, too. They make me pause and wonder what we are doing today. What has the Church become? What is its role in society? How do we, as individuals and as a whole, fare when it comes to helping the poor, to promoting and advocating for social justice, to bringing freedom, to moving into the darkness of addiction, abuse and poverty and to bring light in its stead?

In a letter he wrote from jail in 1963, Dr. Martin Luther King described the Early Church as not only being society's thermometer—reflecting the spiritual and moral state of play—but also the thermostat, raising the heat and changing the air of a watching world. His words were an attempt to encourage the modern-day Church to wake up and take action, to put off self-serving apathy and fight boldly for justice.

There was a time when the church was very powerful—in the time when the early Christians rejoiced at being deemed worthy to suffer for what they believed. In those days the church was not merely a thermometer that recorded the ideas and principles of popular opinion; it was a thermostat that transformed the mores of society. Whenever the early Christians entered a town, the people in power became disturbed and immediately sought to convict the Christians for being "disturbers of the peace" and "outside agitators." But the Christians pressed on, in the conviction that they were "a colony of heaven," called to obey Gad rather than man. Small in number, they were big in commitment. They were too God-intoxicated to be "astronomically intimidated." By their effort and example they brought an end to such ancient evils as infanticide and gladiatorial contests.[1]

He goes on to say some pretty harsh things about the Church:

Things are different now. So often the contemporary church is a weak, ineffectual voice with an uncertain sound. So often it is an archdefender of the status quo.

Far from being disturbed by the presence of the church, the power structure of the average community is consoled by the church's silent—and often even vocal—sanction of things as they are. But the judgment of God is upon the church as never before. If today's church does not recapture the sacrificial spirit of the early church, it will lose its authenticity, forfeit the loyalty of millions, and be dismissed as an irrelevant social club with no meaning for the twentieth century. Every day I meet young people whose disappointment with the church has turned into outright disgust.[2]

What would Dr. King say of us today? Are we a thermostat, are we the agents of change in the world, or are we simply a reflection of its failings? Are we keeping things as they are, or are we hooked in with the change that needs to come? Have we resorted—as I'm afraid some of us sadly have—to being members in an "irrelevant social club"?

What do our songs in church say about us? Are we singing about the world outside those walls, or do we only have words for the nice bits of our relationship with Jesus? Are we able to put into lyrics and music the change that is needed, or can we only talk about ourselves and how warm and fuzzy we feel? Is our soundtrack another example of our making ourselves the center of God's story?

What I know for sure is that on our watch the world has grown hungry as injustice has separated the comfort of "me" from the suffering of "them." We may celebrate the couple of centuries that have passed since slavery was abolished, but can we really be so sure that the world is as free as we would like to believe?

Slavery exists. It comes with real chains as well as invisible ones, but it exists nevertheless. You want proof? Go and see for yourself what life is like for any of the billions who live under the sort of crushing poverty that claims the lives of 25,000 children each day. These people will tell you that their daily struggles between life and death are every bit as hard to break out of as physical chains that bind.

Let's not forget about the real chains of human trafficking: modern-day slavery. From prostitution, begging, forced labor, marriage or illegal adoption, the trade in people is big business. According to Stop The Traffik:

- Two million children are trafficked each year
- At least 12 million people are trapped into forced labor, with as many as 2.4 million of them the victims of human trafficking
- Of all the people trafficked, 80 percent are women and girls
- Trafficking is the second largest source of illegal income worldwide, exceeded only by drug trafficking[3]

The United Nations Declaration of the Rights of the Child—now almost 50 years old—declares that "the child shall be protected against all forms of neglect, cruelty and exploitation. He shall not be subject to traffic, in any form."[4] Something is seriously wrong when such fine words are undermined by the pervasive trafficking of 1.2 million kids a year.

Even though each case of trafficking has its own cruelly unique distinctions, clear patterns emerge: men, women and children, typically from underdeveloped nations, are misled or forcibly removed from their homes and transited to a destination country where they are exploited in some manner. While many victims come from impoverished countries and are therefore vulnerable, naïve and defenseless, victims can also come from wealthy communities and families. Similarly, the slave trade is not localized to poor regions of the world. It is prevalent even in the land of freedom and privilege, such as the United States.

SLAVERY EXISTS. IT COMES WITH REAL CHANGES AS WELL AS INVISIBLE ONES, BUT IT EXISTS NEVERTHELESS.

At the heart of all this talk about action and reaction is a simple question for us: Is a life from a far-away country worth less to us than those of our own? The Bible is clear on its own answer to the question. There, on the cross, arms outspread in tortured welcome to humankind, is Jesus, God's only Son, dying for all, even for the men, women and children all over the globe who never learn His name or see His face.

A few years ago, those WWJD (What Would Jesus Do) bracelets started to get popular. It strikes me that the question posed is fundamentally flawed. We don't need to ask what Jesus *would* do; instead let's ask what He *is doing*. Of the many things we could suggest in answer to the question, here's one that fits perfectly: He's stopping the traffic.

HOPE

We can do better than this. And you know what? I think we *must* do better than this. When Jesus told the assembled people at the synagogue that "the Spirit of the Lord is upon me" (Luke 4:18) to roll out justice and mercy to society's mistreated and forgotten ones, He set the standard for us all. Being agents of justice and love to people in need is not an option to the faith. It's not a take-it-or-leave-it item based on whether or not we feel "called." The call's already been issued; we've been told to go, to love and to serve.

Take a look at your own life. Where do you fit in this picture? Maybe you have already taken steps to form your own history, a legacy you will someday leave behind that shows the fruits of your labor for Christ. Maybe you have some ideas of something you can do. Maybe you are undecided.

Wherever you are in your journey, be encouraged that change is possible. I believe it. I believe it because of what I've read and heard about; because throughout history there have been individuals and groups who have loved and served and lived remarkable lives with remarkable results. Like Margaret Mead once said, "Never doubt that a small group of thoughtful, committed citizens can change the world. Indeed, it's the only thing that ever has."

But my belief in the fact that there are greater things to come—that we don't have to shrug our shoulders and say that the way the world is, is the way the world is—also drives my mind back towards the Church. This was what God has in mind, this was the plan; and not even plan A or plan B, but The Whole Plan. You and me. Us, this beautifully unique collection of 1.4 billion human beings spread across the globe divided by language, theology, wealth, ritual and culture but bound together by grace. We might be well aware of our differences, but we are drawn together by what G. K. Chesterton called "the furious love of God." And that kind of love has a purpose: to bring us closer to Him and to help build His kingdom here on earth. How much greater could things get than that?

We need to be realists. We need to look at the world and see it for how it really is. We need to see the poverty, hear the suffering, peer through the smoke, and see the shackles of injustice and oppression.

We need to be optimists. We need to hear the call of God to believe in the potential of this kingdom getting built by our own hands. We need to accept the value of our calling—to see the role the Church can play in all its glorious fullness, not settle for it as a drab, grey, limp impersonation of a social club. We need to dream and hope and act accordingly. Not for us or our own egos, but for the simple fact that this is all part of the covenant that Jesus made with us on the cross. Forgiveness for sins that allows relationship with God, a relationship that we are compelled to take out and share with the rest of the world. We are blessed to be a blessing and must use that to fuel our forward movement.

We need to be pragmatists. We need to be the sort of people who deal with what needs fixing. We don't need to be picking fights among ourselves or trying to take down imaginary opponents. We need to be dealing with the very people whom Jesus Himself was drawn to—the social outcasts, the poor, the sick, the forgotten, the undesirables, the weak, the oppressed.

Are greater things yet to come? You better believe it. It's just like what Mordecai said to his niece Esther: We might be put where we are in our place in life for a reason (see Esther 4:12-14)—to use our influence and release our potential to build God's kingdom. And we must take on that responsibility however we feel led. I'm pretty sure that if we don't sign up for the job, God will find someone else to do it. Now, I'm all for being generous, but being involved in God's plan to restore hope and justice is one party I'm not going to step away from.

What about you?

FOUR: **READING
THE SIGNS
WRONG**

Let's be honest: It's hard for some people to believe in God. They wrestle with whether or not someone with ties to greatness, goodness and love can allow such suffering in this world. And certainly for those who follow the faith, we have our own questions, our own concerns, our own doubts.

There are certain things the Bible has established about God that I thought of when I was led to write "Greater Things":

- He is the Creator of the Universe (see Gen. 1:1).
- He is the King of kings (see 1 Tim. 6:16).
- He is the strength in our weakness (see 2 Cor. 12:9).
- He is the love to the broken (see Rom. 8:38).
- He is the joy in our sadness (see Ps. 33:11).

These descriptions are weighty pieces of truth, and their meaning goes far beyond the combination of letters used to spell them out. They are too potent to be held in place by just one page. And each of these character traits is like a ball of thread that invites us to pull on the string and see what unravels. If you meditate on these things, I guarantee your wonder and thoughts will widen as you marvel at the astounding truth of what God is like.

Like the fact that He's the Lord of creation, in charge of everything from the beginning to the end. How is that possible? Or the fact that He's the creator, the breath-giver, the life-sustainer, the One who chooses to reveal Himself through a billion complexities in each living thing. Can someone explain how He did it?

Think of a powerful king past or present. God trounces that and any other earthly power of kingship. Any idea how?

He is the strength when we are at our weakest, when we are feeble, when we have lost everything, when we are hanging on the fringed edges of a frayed rope. Can you wrap your mind around this truth?

Then there's the matter of His love for those who are broken, rejected, outcast, ignored, oppressed and abused. Nothing—no situation or person or mistake or evil power—can separate us from His love. It knows no bounds. While we react with our urge to cover up, move on, ignore and wipe clean our problems, they are nothing to God. He does not flinch from a life or family or community or city or nation that is stumbling about in the darkness, torn to pieces from oppression, misfortune or tragedy. Can you explain how that is?

Think about the fact that God is joy. He is not merely fun, amusing, entertaining or good company on a tedious drive. He's joy itself, the very essence of that which transforms life. What do you think about that?

Along with these big statements come big questions. Questions for which most of us have a tough time scrounging up answers. As we experience life, the good and the bad, we may wrestle with our thoughts about God's involvement in life and His character. And sometimes those conversations can lead some of us to confusion, apathy or noninvolvement in building His kingdom. But do you think we have to get rid of all our doubts and questions if we are to move on to the greater things?

BALANCE

Can you imagine what life would be like if we really believed that God was our Lord, our creator, our King, our strength, our love, our joy? How much better off would we be? If we let these words penetrate us to our very core, if we lived with 100 percent belief in their unquestionable truth, then wouldn't our lives be more whole, healthy, purposeful and relatively problem-free? Wouldn't our faith look a hundred times bigger and be more potent if beyond all doubt we knew God to be who He said He is?

Is complete belief and confidence, every second of every day, the code we need to crack in order to "get" Christianity? Do we need to squash our doubt, our questions and our confusion for everything to work out perfectly all the time? Do we have to understand and be well versed in doctrine, theology and hermeneutics to become the sort of Church worthy of the title of Christ's Bride?

Well, that might be true in a perfect world, but it bears no truth in real life. In fact, it's probably a cheap answer, and I'm done with those. The truth for all of us is that there are some gaps in our beliefs. We don't know all the answers, and we should be wary of those who claim they do. We see, as Paul wrote, through a glass darkly (see 1 Cor. 13:12), shrouded in mystery and unable to fully understand this side of heaven.

While there is a permanent tension between faith and doubt, questions and answers, we have to be wise and find a balance. We cannot allow the mystery of our faith and not fully understanding everything to keep us from getting excited or passionate about God and His kingdom. When we do this, we risk upscaling doubt, downgrading our wonder, and reducing God to the role of friendly Uncle. We also cannot live a Pollyanic existence, thinking doubt is not a reality, a fixture of sorts in the journey of faith. Because, let's be honest, suffering exists. Bad stuff happens to good people.

WE CANNOT ALLOW THE MYSTERY OF OUR FAITH AND NOT FULLY UNDERSTANDING EVERYTHING TO KEEP US FROM GETTING EXCITED OR PASSIONATE ABOUT GOD AND HIS KINGDOM.

There is a balance. We don't have to retreat to the margins. We can hold the questions and the faith in the same hand. We can sing about strength in weakness, love in brokenness, and joy in sadness because if you look hard enough, you can see all of the above in evidence around you.

So how do we find the balance between faith and questions? How do we hold pain and hope in the same lives? How do we get better at trusting God?

FAITH ISN'T PERFECT

I know how tough it is to live in a world where evil tramples good, where slavery exists, where poverty keeps light from shining through, where the innocent are slighted, where the widows and orphans get the short end of the stick, where even our own lives are speckled with situations that are unjust, tragic and make no sense. One part of us wants desperately to cling to a God who is loving, and the other part wants to run away because we don't understand how a good God can allow terrible things to happen.

We might as well get something straight: Faith is imperfect in the sense that we don't have it all figured out. None of us have found the foolproof formula of believing, of trusting, of hoping. It's like Emily Dickinson said, "We both believe and disbelieve a hundred times an hour, which keeps believing nimble." Frederick Buechner had the same idea when he wrote, "Doubts are the ants in the pants of faith. They keep it awake and moving."

This delicate dance of faith and doubt is shown in the story of the father with a sick son told in Mark 9. This man is frustrated because when he approaches Jesus' disciples to heal his boy, they aren't able to do anything. They can't heal the kid, and so they send him along to Jesus. The father, at his wits' end, cries out, "Have mercy on us and help us, if you can" (Mark 9:22, NLT). That's when Jesus poses an important question: "What do you mean, 'If I can'? . . . Anything is possible if a person believes" (Mark 9:23, NLT).

The answer to this question is crucial in seeing where the distraught father is coming from, what lies at the core of his heart, what he really believes. The guy responds in a way that is telling, sobering and true for most of us who are honest in our faith journey: "I do believe, but help me overcome my unbelief" (Mark 9:24, *NLT*). In other words, "I believe (sigh), but there's a little part of me that wonders, that questions, that toys with doubt." You know what happened with the sick boy? Jesus healed him. Clearly Jesus is well aware of and understands the implication of the marriage of belief and unbelief. And clearly He doesn't think we "don't get it" when our faith doesn't measure up to an impossible standard of perfection.

Make no mistake: Although our faith is fluid, we are still called to trust in God. Though we may live with some gaps, more questions than answers, and imperfect faith, we must let God be God and submit to His authority. We must surrender to accepting that, yes, even in a world that is messy, He can work through muck and mire for good. He can bring great things to our cities. He can intervene in our causes even though the trusting part may feel a little shaky.

WHAT IS TRUST?

I trust you to do what you've said.

I can trust them to sort it out.

I'll trust her to be there for me.

I trust the rope to take my weight.

I can trust the driver to get me there safely.

We use trust in a specific way, as one half of an equation, always linked to an outcome. We use it like the ink on a contract; we assume it's there for a clearly defined purpose.

This might work out okay when we're buying a house or planning a vacation, but is that the way we need to be with God? Are we really comfortable assuming that our trust in Him can be withheld until He sets out precisely to make us happy, fulfill our wishes, and answer our prayers?

Remember Jesus' disciple Thomas? He used the same sort of contract when he missed out on one of the most astounding encounters with Jesus that the Bible describes. His friends had locked themselves away in a room, frightened about what the Jews might do to them. Out of nowhere, Jesus appeared right there in front of them, offering peace, forgiveness and breathing on them to gift the Holy Spirit. It was, and still is, one of the most incredible encounters of all time (see John 20:19-23).

But where was Thomas? We don't know where he was, but we do know that he wasn't there. Perhaps he was less afraid of what the Jews would do to Jesus' friends and was braver than the rest. Perhaps he was bolder than the others. We don't know for sure, but we do know that the Gospels are pretty clear about what happened when he found out about missing out on seeing Jesus. He was upset and started to throw around some pretty big statements: Unless I get some physical proof for myself—unless I can see those wounds—I won't believe. Unless X happens, then I simply will not believe. Because Jesus didn't fit into my plot, He's going to have to change, not me (see John 20:24-25).

Thomas's faith was conditional. His trust came with a price tag. His belief was bound up in legalism.

It's funny, but when he finally gets to see the risen Jesus face to face, John doesn't say whether Thomas actually does go ahead and touch and feel Jesus' wounds for himself. He could have touched them—no doubt about it—but I get the feeling that, standing face to face with Jesus, calling him out of his unbelief, Thomas suddenly knows that his grand statement is now sounding a little hollow.

Sometimes that's what happens to us. We lock ourselves up with the idea that we can only trust in God if certain things happen and God breaks through. Sometimes all our grand ideas and clever assumptions get exposed for the weakness and foolishness they really are. Sometimes we're just too bound up in our own plots to allow Jesus to rewrite the rules.

WHAT DOES FAITH LOOK LIKE?

When a friend of mine found out that his wife was pregnant with their fourth child, he was thrilled, but not overly ecstatic about the whole thing. He told me that he would wait on getting super excited about it, as he'd learned from the other three pregnancies that nine months was a long time to wait to meet the little one.

But their previous three experiences were nothing like this one. His wife started bleeding around the time when bleeding usually signifies a miscarriage. To make matters a little more complicated, he and his wife were just emerging out of a year of emotional upheaval: both of their mothers, as well as my friend's stepfather, had died from cancer within a five-month period.

So it's not surprising that when all this bleeding started, the couple feared the worst. Was this pregnancy heading in a different direction than the others? Were they heading for death and flowers and cards and kind words and self-imposed hibernation from much of life?

The night before his wife was scheduled for an ultrasound, a friend came to see them. She told them that perhaps God might be saying that, just like the previous year when they'd lost their mothers and stepdad, they needed to surrender all and simply trust God again.

My friend was unimpressed by her advice. As far as he could see it, there was no way that the baby could have survived all that bleeding. Trust? Surrender? It just didn't make any sense. The only thing he could surrender was all hope of the baby surviving. As for trust, they both knew from experience that God could be trusted to be there, no matter how great the sorrow. They could trust God, but that didn't mean trusting that God would make the baby live.

Later, as this couple was lying in bed at night, something shifted. My friend turned on the light and said softly to his wife, "You don't think we're supposed to surrender our pessimism as well, do you? And what about our trust? Are we meant to trust in something other than God getting us through another loss?"

His wife didn't reply at first. Staring off into the distance, she remembered the times when God had felt close: at the funerals of the year before, holding the hand of her mother as she lay dying in front of her, taking communion together as the cancer took charge and prepared for its final assault.

God had been there. He had been there in the fear and in the grief that followed. He had never let go. But could He rewrite the script? Could He make this bleeding something other than a miscarriage?

My friend's wife slept and dreamed of the way the sun feels on one's skin at the start of a hot day. The next morning, it took the sonographer all of 10 seconds to get a fix on the baby and proclaim it perfectly healthy.

Can we trust God to rewrite the script? Can we allow a different ending other than the one we're convinced lies ahead of us? Can we surrender our need for proof or equations or conditional responses from God? Can we put all of this aside and trust with open hearts? If we can get better at this, then our path ahead will start to look a whole lot brighter.

WHAT DOES GOD WANT FROM US?

Sometimes we do the same thing in situations that force us to face the challenge of trusting God. We trust Him, but only so far as we can throw Him. Our trust is bound up with assumptions, expectations and prescribed notions of exactly what that trust will deliver into our laps.

While this is a normal reaction, feeding this attitude will only produce more doubts and prevent our faith from growing. Whenever we talk about "trust" here, we're talking about "faith" as well; the willful act of choosing to follow God's lead rather than forge our own path.

Some of us might assume that faith is a gift; one of those things that you either have or you don't, like a full head of hair or the ability to sleep through thunderstorms. Is that true? Do you think God just chooses the lucky ones and leaves the rest of us lacking in the faith department?

Nice possibility, but it doesn't wash. The Bible is loaded with examples of people who needed to nurture and deepen their faith, not a special elite bunch who were born having a lot of faith all the time. It's also not about binging on faith to see what we can get out of it. Faith is something else entirely.

There's a great story told about Moses in Exodus 17. There he is, on top of a hill watching the battle between the Israelites and the Amalekites. There is a strange formula in place that determines the winner of this fight. As long as Moses keeps his hands up, his people find themselves winning. As soon as his hands drop, they take a beating. Moses eventually grows tired. His arms must feel like lead, and so his brother, Aaron, and Hur, one of the kings of Midian, prop him up and hold his arms up for him. The Israelites defeat their enemy, and Moses builds an altar on the battleground and calls it "The Lord is my banner" (see Exod. 17:15).

What a great picture of faith and trust this is. We're not left feeling impressed with Moses' biceps or even his tenacity. What gets me is that it's a great example of unity; three leaders gathered together to achieve a greater thing than either could have managed on their own. You could also say it's an illustration of how the small steps we take are often all that's needed to allow God to work through us. Then again, you could point to the symbolism of the story; three men standing together, one on the right, the other on the left, acting as one and influencing the battle taking place before them.

Whatever lesson you take away from this story, it is almost impossible to ignore the central message that the writer was getting across: If we want to know the Lord as our "banner," we will have to take some risks (in other words, have a little faith) and whatever steps (sometimes logical, sometimes odd) that will get us where He wants us.

So, having faith and trust in God is kind of practical. It's not all about believing in fairies, happily-ever-after endings, and warm and fuzzy feelings. It's about digging our heels into what we believe God is calling us to do and strengthening whatever bit of faith we have to watch it grow.

HAVING FAITH AND TRUST IN GOD IS ABOUT DIGGING OUR HEELS INTO WHAT WE BELIEVE GOD IS CALLING US TO DO AND STRENGTHENING WHATEVER BIT OF FAITH WE HAVE TO WATCH IT GROW.

There is a well-known verse about Abraham that says "he believed the LORD, and he [God] credited it to him as righteousness" (Gen. 15:6). Because this man had faith, God was happy. Right? Is that it? Does that mean we have to rid our minds of doubt and purge ourselves of any unbelief in order to please God and guarantee a favorable outcome?

It's not hard to see why this kind of thinking would appeal to most of us. After all, if the key to life being fine and dandy is simply believing enough, then how hard can it be? Ask any diehard fan of a struggling sports team and they'll tell you that finding belief in the midst of failure isn't so hard after all.

But following God is not like standing on a damp, empty touchline week after week. It's not about denying the evidence or ignoring the facts. It's not about abandoning our questions or faking the feelings.

The Hebrew word for "believe" in that verse in Genesis is 'aman, which literally means to build up, to support, and to nurture. That doesn't mean that God liked Abraham because he put a Band-Aid over God's booboo, but that the kind of faith and trust Abraham had was the kind that grows and needs care, support and nurturing. In other words, Abraham had to work out his faith.

Skip forward to Job 39, and we see that 'aman word translated again, but this time in a way that sheds more light on its meaning. The *King James Version* keeps 'aman as "believe," and it sounds a little weird: "He swalloweth the ground with fierceness and rage: neither believeth he that it is the sound of the trumpet" (Job 39:24).

Take a more modern translation, and you get a clearer picture with this new meaning of the word: "With shaking and rage he races over the ground, and he does not stand still at the voice of the trumpet" (*NASB*).

"Stand still." It's as simple as that. Faith, trust and belief in God is often a matter of us simply standing still, standing firm, standing our ground in the face of all manner of opposition.

So, what does all this faith and trust in God have to do with anything? It matters. A lot. If we are really to believe that God can use us to impact the world for change; that the suffering of the poor, the abandoned, the addict, the lost, the abused and the rejected can be alleviated; and that hope can be restored in our lives, our homes, our communities and our cities, then we are going to have to keep the faith. We are going to have to believe in God as ruler of all, giver of strength to the weak, love to the broken, and joy to those who mourn.

God does not ask us to simply shout that we believe or put on a nice smile as our badge of faith. It's not a fake-it-until-you-make-it attitude that He is asking of us. He wants us to stand our ground, to nurture our belief and allow it to grow in community with Him as well as our fellow believers.

Stand firm.

Over time.

With God and others.

That's what true faith is.

Remember how I said that our faith is imperfect? Well, believing God in the way He is asking of us does not suggest that we should sweep all our questions under the carpet. Abraham didn't. Read Genesis 18 when you get a chance. There you'll find the "father of faith" asking God to change His mind about some serious stuff, specifically on what basis God will destroy the city of Sodom. Who says God wants us to be silent puppets who don't inquire of Him?

We need this kind of faith to live in the real world. None of this makes sense without having something to stand firm *against*, or having struggles, or wrestling with the temptation to take things into our own hands and bail on God and others. God doesn't call us out of the realities of life to live some plasticized existence. When we want to see great things happen, it's only going to happen when we grow in faith—the kind of faith that is strengthened in the presence of pain, struggles and trials that require us to stand firm.

FINDING OUR FEET

It certainly wasn't my first test of faith—and it surely won't be my last—but finding out that my three-week-old daughter, Lily, had cystic fibrosis was, well, difficult.

My wife, Jill, and I were first-time parents, and ever since our daughter's birth, our world had been rocked, just like people told us it would. The raging hormones, the lack of sleep, the excitement, the rush of having seen Jill go through labor— it all left our heads buzzing. Everything was different now, and chaos was the new normal.

We started seeing unusual signs as we cared for our newborn girl, but we never gave them much thought. Why wouldn't we be going through 15 to 20 diapers a day? Wasn't that what everyone else did? And we knew that babies' body weight dipped after birth, so we weren't surprised when Lily's did as well. But it kept on going down. And down. That's when we started to wonder what was going on.

The doctors did some tests. It turned out that Lily's salt levels were high, and what with all the pooping and the weight loss, all signs pointed to cystic fibrosis. It's a hereditary disease that affects the internal organs, especially the lungs and digestive system, by clogging them with thick, sticky mucus. This makes it hard to breathe and digest food. The average life expectancy for a person diagnosed with the illness is 31.

I was away at a conference when the results from the final tests came through. It was confirmed. Lily had it.

"Don't go browsing through the Internet," the nurse warned. She said that doing so would only freak us out, as there were a plethora of scare stories out there as well as a handful of questionable charities trying to increase their fundraising by upping the fear factor. The nurse wanted me to come into the hospital the next day to talk further. For some reason, I just knew that I couldn't go home. I needed to stay where I was and continue to lead worship at the conference as planned.

It wasn't about me being a macho man or claiming some kind of weird kudos for keeping my schedule. I knew I had a choice: I could stay and sing with all my heart or leave immediately and retreat to the fear. I could surround myself with others, leaning on them for support where I was, or I could get back in the car on my own and allow my thoughts to run rampant.

A couple of days later, the event was over and my wife and I were in the clinic finding out more with the doctors.

"Will she have to spend the rest of her life in a baby carriage?" I asked.

"No."

"Is it as serious as people think?"

"It's really serious. In the past, kids didn't live past the age of five, but we have made some medical advancements. Now there are 12-year-olds having lung transplants. It can't be cured—or rather they can't get the cure to work quite yet; those antibodies just can't seem to stick. Not yet."

"But will they?"

"I think they will."

I wondered to myself, *Will Lily be healed?* I believe the answer to be yes.

Lily's four now, and you know what? She is doing fine. More than fine, even.

As I'm learning things as we go forward, the lessons are beginning to sink in. I don't believe that God wants Lily to be sick. I think sometimes we get confused about sickness and salvation. Here's what I mean. In Mark 5, Jesus is in full physical healing mode, helping not only the demon-possessed man but also a dead girl and a sick woman. The father of the dying girl asks Jesus, "Please come and lay your hands on her; heal her so she can live" (Mark 5:23, *NLT*). The sick woman stuck in a swarm of people trying to get close to Jesus tells herself, "If I can just touch his robe, I will be healed" (Mark 5:28, *NLT*).

I like how N.T. Wright translates these two verses in *Surprised by Hope*. According to the Greek, the word "heal" means more than what we think; its definition can shift the sky and open up the heavens. It translates into the word "save."

"Please come and lay your hands on her; save her so she can live."

"If I can just touch his robe, I will be *saved*."

Salvation isn't just limited to what happens to us after we die; it's caught up in elements of the present just as much as it is in the eternal. There are physical aspects of salvation that we can seek today, just as the crowds around Jesus did a long time ago.

Another thing: When Jesus heals, He's not just handing out goodies or extra treats for the ones He notices. He's not rewarding the folks with the loudest voices or the strongest grip. He's bringing on the greater things to all people.

God is bringing to the here and now elements of His salvation that will make our lives better here on earth. That means the sick can be cared for, the poor can be fed, the lonely can be comforted, the broken can be healed. God can do all these things for all of us.

I believe that Lily will be healed, just as I believe that if I care about the eternal salvation of anyone else on the planet, I should care about his or her physical condition as well.

HERE'S WHAT I BELIEVE . . .

You have to ask yourself why we're not seeing so many of those greater things as we'd like. I know sometimes we can blame ourselves and feel as if God has abandoned us in this call when we compare ourselves to the big player in church. What's wrong with us? Why aren't we making the A team?

That's where the problem starts. Like I've said before, when we make this story about us—when we put ourselves in the driving seat and director's chair—we end up making a mockery of God.

At times like that, we make trust and faith and believing in God into something far different than what it's supposed to be. We make it about the noise we create, about the extent to which we can block out negatives, or—most crazy of all—a measure of our own greatness. If we can overcome some of this, if we can learn to spot the traps and avoid them before we're snared, we might find ourselves facing a slightly altered state of play:

A world where our questions don't rule us out.

A world where salvation means good news to people right here, right now, as well as after death.

A world that doesn't see the Church in retreat but advancing forward, no matter the cost.

FIVE: **SIGNS THAT POINT TO GOD**

Believing in the goodness, omnipotence, glory and faithfulness of God means sticking with Him through whatever comes at us. In whatever situation we find ourselves—whether we are enduring pain, stress or even learning a life lesson the hard way, God is to be trusted. Let's be honest: It's usually in those kinds of situations where we learn the greatest lessons and our faith is strengthened. And, yes, I do know that sometimes that is easier said than done.

FINDING MEANING IN THE STRUGGLE

Depending on how you choose to look at it, being a Christian in China at the turn of the last century was one of two extremes: either good or bad. Reacting to decades of territorial infiltration by foreign powers and the presence and influence of missionary evangelism, the extreme nationalist group known as the Boxers gathered momentum at the end of 1900. Uniting under the slogan "Support the Qing and destroy the foreigners," they launched a rebellion that, although eventually overthrown, left an audacious body count in their wake. About 200 foreign missionaries and 32,000 Chinese Christians were slaughtered for their faith during this uprising.

It's not hard to see why this was tragic. There's no other way to describe the senseless murders. But there's another face to that brutal massacre that reflects courage, strength and an unwavering faith tested beyond what you can imagine. I think about the story of the one Chinese pastor who refused to recant his faith. Incensed by his stand, the mob cut off his eyebrows, lips and ears. When he continued to stand his ground and still refused to deny his faith, they cut his heart out of his body. The pastor's 14-year-old daughter witnessed the bloodshed but didn't let it move her. She, too, refused to turn her back on Christ, sharing her father's fate as well as his faith.

Intent on ridding their land of the "white devils," the Boxers rampaged the cities of north China and killed as many Christians as they could. They tied one pastor to a pillar inside a pagan temple. All night, the man preached to his captors. Morning brought with it an angry mob 1,000 strong. The crowd tore this man's heart out.

That same crowd in Tsun-hua chopped the feet off an uncooperative Chinese Christian teacher. While her colleague was being burned alive, she implored her pupils to "keep the faith."

Do you feel the power of unrelenting faith here? Isn't there something about the sacrifice these martyrs made that is sobering and inspiring, forcing us to ask how far we would go for our own beliefs? The nineteenth-century Polish poet Cyprian Norwid understood this. According to him, a truly fulfilling life must contain three essential requirements: "something to live on, something to live for, and something to die for. The lack of one of these attributes results in drama. The lack of two results in tragedy."

It would be ridiculous to view the suffering of these persecuted Christians as punishment or as a consequence of some monumental failure on their part. It might be hard to believe, but isn't this kind of pain, torment and torture in fact a vehicle for proving the incredible faith of these believers and the greatness of God's own sacrifice for us?

I think so.

I truly believe that all kinds of struggle—the times when our easy answers just don't seem to fit in any way, when injustice wreaks senseless havoc, when what we believe is stretched to unimaginable lengths—can often be the times when our faith comes alive. It is also a place where we are drawn closer to God.

The early Christians knew this. Perhaps it had something to do with the persecution binges the Church had to endure under various emperors and rulers who made killing them a national sport. Nero used to crucify Christians and then set their bodies on fire to serve as human candles to light his garden parties. I suppose that living with the potential of that happening forces you to make up your mind as to what you really believe. After all, it was something at that time believers knew could cost them their lives.

These Christians—the earliest expressions of the Church—found life in death. They weren't afraid of it. They didn't treat it like it would never happen. It wasn't at all unusual for them to meet together in cemeteries, gathering around the tomb of a loved one on the anniversary of his or her birth or death. They'd share a meal together—one where the ingredients were chosen to represent life in its fullest: fish, bread, cakes and wine. They weren't being morbid (as many of us would assume); these men and women simply viewed death in a different light than we do today.

For them death was not the be-all-end-all, nor was it a sign of God's absence. As they poured wine over the tomb, the believers would call out *"vibas!"* (live!), uniting them and their dead loved one together. They were not limited, severed or depressed by the reality of death or suffering. They grew on the inside because of it.

So what's our deal? Why do we often think that because we have been met by hardship or strife in life it is because we have failed in some way, or let God down, or have fallen out of His good grace?

There are many people out there who will tell you that you are going through something difficult because there is something wrong with your faith or you just don't have enough of it. Well, they're wrong. Suffering is not evidence of God's punishment, frustration, weakness or boredom. Challenges, difficulties and pain are a part of life (go ahead, find someone who has not been through a tough time in his or her life). Not only that, but it's our opportunity to exercise who we are in Christ and show the world that we are "more than conquerors" (Rom. 8:37) and that God is greater than the evils of this world (see 1 John 4:4).

As I write this, the world is in terrible economic shape. People everywhere are freaking out because jobs are being lost, homes are being foreclosed, and bank accounts are dwindling. Anxiety is at an all-time high because our finances and, therefore, things such as maintaining a lifestyle of excess to being able to pay bills to affording health insurance for our kids are being threatened. Some of us are allowing this trying time to drive a wedge between us and God.

But are these fears all they're cracked up to be?

Are we more focused on life in this crisis than on the darkness?

Are we convinced that we will not recover from this trial?

May we remember the words of Paul, a missionary who had been through persecution, shipwrecks, illness and imprisonment:

"We are pressed on every side by troubles, but we are not crushed. We are perplexed, but not driven to despair. We are hunted down, but never abandoned by God. We get knocked down, but we are not destroyed. Through suffering, our bodies continue to share in the death of Jesus so that the life of Jesus may also be seen in our bodies" (2 Cor. 4:8-10, *NLT*).

WE MUST PERSIST IN BUILDING GOD'S KINGDOM EVEN WHEN WE EXPERIENCE LOSS, OBSTACLES, POOR HEALTH, PERSECUTION AND WHEN OUR WORLD IS SHIFTED UPSIDE DOWN.

May we also be strengthened by the examples the Early Church martyrs left at their deaths. May they remind us that we are able to draw closer to God through suffering. We don't need to bail on Him. We don't need to give up when met with resistance. We must carry on. We must persist in building His kingdom, even when we experience loss, obstacles, poor health, persecution and when our world is shifted upside down.

LET GOD BE GOD

So much of life these days is far removed from literal life and death decisions. Having something to die for seems more relevant to buying the latest pair of chic shoes (sorry, girls!) than something truly important. It seems as though we spend more time worrying about playlists and pensions than persecution and prayer. Some of us might be treating lightly the religious freedoms that we enjoy; I know for sure that being able to practice my faith in public is a massive privilege (growing up a Christian in a city where people are killing each other because of their faith will do that for you).

This is another reminder not to align ourselves with what our culture dictates is a superficial or inward-focused priority or necessity. We must align ourselves with God and what He deems should rank over everything else: loving and serving Him and others.

Part of putting our faith into action means allowing God to be God. It means allowing God to work in every space in our lives—the good and the bad. If we're too busy filling up our lives with only ourselves, what room is there for God to work through us? And while television, magazines and advertisements tell us that life begins and ends with our desires, Pope John Paul II had a better idea when he said that faith leads us beyond ourselves. And so it should.

When we partner with God and abandon our selfishness, it teaches us the value of taking seriously His commands, like the one in Deuteronomy 15:4 where God's chosen people are told that there should be no one poor living among them. The Israelites were given strict instructions on how to achieve such a utopian state—debts were cancelled every seven years, the edges of fields were left unharvested so that the poor could glean the remaining crops, the people were to maintain generous and giving attitudes to those in need.

It's practical and simple advice, all concerned with being a little less selfish. This is the same kind of mentality we have to have to make great things happen. To heal our lands from poverty, slavery and injustice requires us to be more selfless. It leads us beyond ourselves by forcing us to open our eyes to the struggle that our neighbor down the street or across the ocean is going through. It pushes us to ask the question, "What can we do to make things better?"

GOD'S BACK

I read Exodus 33 the other day and I can't get it out of my mind.

The passage tells the story of when Moses practically begs God to show Himself as he is leading the people of Israel out of slavery and into the Promised Land. Moses is convinced that if God will do that for him, then His people will know for sure that He is with them and is giving them His favor. God agrees, but on one condition: Moses cannot look at His face.

> "I will make all my goodness pass before you, and I will call out my name, Yahweh, before you. For I will show mercy to anyone I choose, and I will show compassion to anyone I choose. But you may not look directly at my face, for no one may see me and live." The LORD continued, "Look, stand near me on this rock. As my glorious presence passes by, I will hide you in the crevice of the rock and cover you with my hand until I have passed by. Then I will remove my hand and let you see me from behind. But my face will not be seen" (Exod. 33:19-23, *NLT*).

God would only allow Moses to see His back. Doesn't that seem a little odd? Can God have a back and, if He does, does it also mean that He has a top, a bottom and a front? Does God having a back mean He has a distinctive shape? It's fascinating to think about, isn't it?

Rabbi Lawrence Kushner wrote a poignant reflection on his perspective of this event:

> The Hebrew word for "my back" is *achorai*. . . . The word *achor* also has a temporal sense. What God seems to be saying to Moses is that you can see "my afterward." You can see just what it's like after I've been here. But if you knew what it was like while I was still there, that would mean you were still hanging on to a little piece of your self-awareness that was telling you it was you who was there. And that would also mean there was a part of your consciousness detached and watching the whole thing and therefore not *all of you* was there. There are, in other words, simply some things in life that demand such total self absorption that you cannot know it's you who is there until it's over. Being in the presence of God is such an experience.[1]

Here's what this means to me. In life, we are often impatient. We spend so much of our time wanting to be able to see the full picture, to find reason or logic behind life's challenges and hardships, to understand the answer to our deepest questions. We want answers to the eternal questions of why. Why me? Why this? Why now?

Perhaps in the rush to get past the struggles, pain and suffering, we miss out on what is to be gained from being in the middle of it.

Perhaps by glossing over the weakness, the sadness and the brokenness, we miss out on the strength, the love, the joy.

Perhaps in our desire to have life mapped out, we end up getting ourselves horribly lost.

Perhaps in our climb to figure out the formula for life, we realize there is none.

Perhaps it would be better if we just allowed ourselves to be with God and trust Him in the middle of the darkest times.

MODERN—DAY PHARISEES

The Pharisees had a tough time of letting God be God in their lives. The core of their being was soaked in legalism—following rules and looking good on the outside. Instead of allowing religion to bring about transformation and help them be people who paid attention to the physical and spiritual needs of others, they used it as a tool to make themselves look good. They wanted nothing to do with the message of compassion, service, mercy and love that Jesus brought. They just wanted the glory of representing the spiritually elite leaders in society.

Just as God can use suffering to bring people closer to Him or to bring them to the depths of true faith, He can do the same thing by bringing to light our false or misconceived notions of faith.

Case in point: Jesus ripped into the Pharisees time after time. Why? To make them feel bad? To condemn them? No. I believe it was because He loved them and wanted them to come to an understanding that how they viewed spirituality was backward. If He didn't give a hoot about the state of their spiritual health, He would have left them alone. But Jesus did care. He was constantly bringing to light what they hid in secret to show them they had a skin-deep view of religion.

I used to really like the passage in Matthew where Jesus uses razor-sharp language when He calls the Pharisees snakes. "You brood of snakes! How could evil men like you speak what is good and right? For whatever is in your heart determines what you say" (Matt. 12:34, *NLT*). I liked it, but for all the wrong reasons. Maybe it had something to do with growing up where I did, but I loved the "them and us" tone of the passage. I loved the thought of Jesus playing Rabbi Rambo, taking down the *uber*-religious with some seriously loaded words.

Now I like it for a different reason; it has so much meaning for us today. There is no doubt that Jesus still gets offended by false displays of religion, and there are plenty of modern-day Pharisees who are alive and well. Just look at what He was criticizing them for and compare their behaviors to Christians you may know.

Jesus repeatedly called them hypocrites, fools and liars. In Matthew 23 in particular, Jesus delivered an impassioned monologue directed at these guys. He accused them of pursuing the law and little else, caring more for following Temple rules than caring for orphans or widows. The Pharisees confused the outward signs of religious observance with the internal quest to serve and follow our heavenly Father. They fell for the age-old lie that if things look okay on the outside, they look the same within. They missed the mark that spirituality is about the pursuit of God; it is a personal affair, not a corporate exercise in impressing others or getting as much out for yourself as is possible.

As well as their legalistic attitude, Jesus had a go at their piety. The Pharisees had a habit of saying that had they been around in the years gone by, they would have played no part in the murder of the prophets. They believed they were incapable of wrongdoing and that it was what set them apart from the regular folk. Know any modern-day Pharisees like that? People who say things like, "I would never say that." "I would never go there." "I would never say those things." Jesus continued His rampage, accusing the Pharisees of being hypocritical, greedy, getting what they can out of people, regardless of how bad a deal they offer. Their morality was weak, they were self-indulgent, they were flaky; they were the sort of people who know what they should do but fail to do it anyway.

I'll be honest. This passage scares me. I see how explicit Jesus is in where these leaders have gone wrong. It raps at the door of my own conscience. I think of the hypocrisy, greed and immorality that are going around, even in my own life. Is Jesus accusing us of those same things? Are we just as guilty today in how we act, what we do or don't do, or how we prioritize our lives as the Pharisees were back then?

As a worship leader, I especially think about the words we sing in church. Are we living out what we sing about outside those four walls? When we sing things like, "giving all I am," "I surrender all," "I live for you," what do we really mean? Are we putting those melodic lyrics into action? Are we carrying out God's purpose in our families, our neighborhoods, our communities, our cities, our world?

Are we free from greed? Do we hoard our money or give generously to God through our churches and charities to the poor and needy? Are we free from hypocrisy? Do we practice what we preach within our homes and at work? Are we free from foolish behavior? Do we paint gray over the black-and-white issues of sin so we can do what we want?

ARE WE LIVING OUT WHAT WE SING ABOUT OUTSIDE OF THE FOUR WALLS OF THE CHURCH? ARE WE CARRYING OUT GOD'S PURPOSE IN OUR WORLD?

Surely we're okay on the business front, right? I mean, which of us is turning the screws on poor workers? It's not as if you or I own a sweat shop, right? Which of us is part of the chain that leaves people virtual slaves, forced to work in conditions that are so sub-standard as to be criminally negligent? Did you hear about the company in India that—in order to maximize productivity, increase competitiveness, and win a lucrative western contract—placed extra sewing stations across the fire doors of its third-story factory? When the inevitable fire came, a dozen workers, all of them women, and most of them mothers, died. Who among us would support them? I wouldn't. Would you? But then again, where did those cheap jeans I bought the other week come from? What corners were cut to make the price so temptingly low?

And just who are our banks lending our money out to? How are those farmers treated? What was the impact on the local communities of the 15 gallons of fuel we just shoved in our tank?

We may not work in the business world, but like it or not, we're all in the business of employing people. Although there might be thousands of miles between the till and the sweatshop floor, we are still responsible for how we spend our money. As socially conscious Christians, the gospel that Jesus preached, we need to start paying attention to the world around us and not focus only on the people in church, or those in our Bible study, or our friends in our small group.

The harsh words that Jesus gave to the Pharisees are not a glimpse into a long-distant past. Their problems are our problems. These are the same old issues and slip-ups and sins that we've been falling down on since . . . well, since forever.

Close your eyes and imagine yourself as Jesus delivers His rant. How do you feel? What are you thinking? What does your body language say? Is there anyone who could possibly imagine standing in front of Jesus with a smirk and arms crossed as the Pharisees finally got what was coming to them? I know I would be hoping beyond all hope that it wasn't going to be me that Jesus would point to next. I'd be recalling and confessing about as fast as I possibly could, hoping that in the weird physics of it, Jesus would somehow be too busy with His speech to notice that He was also hearing my confession.

LOVE THROUGH REVELATION

Why were the Pharisees there in the first place? Yes, there were probably a hundred different reasons why they were gathered. Some were there to trick, some to spy, some to connect, some to ogle, some to believe, some to repent. In truth, we will never know why they were there. But we do know this: Jesus wanted to connect with them.

We should not fall into the trap of thinking that because Jesus' words are strong, His heart is therefore cold to the Pharisees. I believe that Jesus' emotions are high not just because of their sin but also because time was running out, because the cycle of religiosity had to be broken, because He needed to get across that true faith has to do with a transformation of the heart. Jesus was adamant about communicating that loving and serving God had nothing to do with following the law as closely as possible.

Jesus wasn't embarrassed by or threatened by these legalistic individuals. He just knew that having this attitude wasn't going to bridge the gap between humankind and God. Jesus was on His way to the cross to make that happen. He was on His way to taking on the wickedness of the world and exhausting it. Jesus was making clear to the Pharisees their guilt—everything from their narrow-mindedness to their hypocrisy—because without such an awareness of what they were doing wrong, Jesus' steps to the cross, His death and resurrection would make absolutely no sense at all. Without this wake-up call, they would struggle to accept His ultimate sacrifice.

Jesus was lashing the Pharisees with the truth about their failings not to condemn them but to do the very opposite: to save and redeem them because He loved them. It's like He said, "O Jerusalem . . . How often I have wanted to gather your children together as a hen protects her chicks beneath her wings, but you wouldn't let me" (Matt. 23:37, *NLT*). Sadly, they never let Jesus scoop them up into His arms; they fell into the trap of resisting Him.

The miracle of the relationship that Jesus offers us is not that He loves us *in spite* of our sin—that implies God would (and could) love us more if only we could sin a little less. Hear the truth: God's love could not be any fiercer or bolder or brighter or stronger for us than it is right now. Regardless of what our Internet browser, bank statements, friends or utterly over-inflated sense of self might suggest, God could not love us more than He does today.

God couldn't love you more.

It was the same for the Pharisees. It was His love that drove Him to them, His love that fired His anger, His love that scarred His heart.

But that love gets held at bay when we refuse to accept the fact that we are in desperate need of it. Without waking up to our sin, Jesus' death looks like nothing more than martyrdom, rough-justice or foolish self-sacrifice. Without acknowledging that we have got it wrong, we hold back from true redemption for ourselves and, ultimately, the unfolding of how we can make a difference for others.

Think about Jesus on the cross, arms nailed in welcome to all who approach Him. We cannot come closer to Jesus without noticing the suffering that put Him there on the cross, and we cannot ignore the nails, the blood, the pain. Through Christ's suffering we are given life—a new chance at living with purpose, with mercy and with the capacity to make the world around us a better one.

COMING CLEAN

We need this today. We might be shielding ourselves with the legalism of "being in the club" already or trying to get away with just showing up enough in church, but it won't do. It won't do for God, and it won't do for us.

Let's remember the accusations thrown at the Pharisees, in particular the one about whitewashed tombs that hid grime and dirt, and think about the toxic mix of spiritual apathy and sin that we'd rather keep hidden. We must not fall into the same trap, taking shelter behind a mask while at the same time nurturing the very things that cloud our view and cover us from the love of God.

Some of us are better at creating the façade, some of our masks are bigger or more elaborate than others, and some of us have deeper, darker secrets. Whether we are concealing our true identity, closet skeletons or lusts by fig leaves or a persona of the "Perfect Christian," one thing is for certain: Jesus is calling us out. He knows our game. There's no point in hiding anymore. The scheme is up. He's found us out.

Some of this can make us feel uncomfortable. We don't like reading or hearing about things that make us feel bad. But if we flip that statement over, are we really so sure that the main purpose of our faith is to feel good about ourselves, even if we are in need of transformation? Is true religion designed solely to make us feel cozy?

Yes, there is grace. Yes, there is hope. And, yes, there is the protection of the mother hen gathering her chicks under her wings, but we need to have God's light shine into our darker places so we can become the people He has created us to be.

This is how we can see that same light shed to all dark places throughout the world.

WHERE GOD IS

Some people have a misconstrued sense of the coupling of faith and life. They'll tell you that suffering is caused by a lack of faith. They'll say that weakness is a sign of failure. They'll tell you that the world is made up of *them* and *us*; that God's love resides over here, with us, His chosen ones, while those on the other side remain alone, without blessing and without hope. They hand out judgment like grandmas hand out candies, but have nothing to say about grace.

Have you ever met someone who has been through something horrendous but somehow seems to have grown through the experience? Perhaps he or she has known the weight of grief or the pain of separation, or it could have been the long, hard slog of chronic pain or heartbreak. Yet somehow—and not *in spite of*, but almost *because of* these struggles—he or she has become more alive. Maybe you are that person and you know exactly what I'm talking about. Maybe you need to meet someone like this to prompt some energy back into your faith.

The truth about suffering and pain and weakness and all those things that look ugly and messy is that they are not the signs of failure and chaos and trouble. Just like the Pharisees' guilt, they can be the exact route that leads us closer to God.

Are you feeling weak? That's where we find God's strength.

Are you feeling broken? The door to God's love is already opening.

Are you sad, overwhelmed, or stressed? There's joy there, too.

Not only can we trust God in suffering, but we can also learn something when we see suffering in others. The suffering in this world can be a way for us to live out the love of God that we have pled allegiance to. It can be the channel for God to roll out the greater things.

SIX: SMILES

It's those smiles that do it. They are complex and not easy to read at all, but the smiles of the girls in Pattaya that worked as prostitutes, strippers, escorts and whatever else left an impression on me.

They were beautiful.

They were fake.

They were plastered on and painted up and handed out with the aim of selling sex.

But was that all they could ever be? Were these girls caught up in the sex trade destined to live a life of abuse, misuse and shame? Was this all there was for them? I didn't believe it. I saw behind the smiles to the potential that each of those women had. I knew God saw bigger for them than their occupation. I knew God saw greater in them than making a buck off of people's lust. I knew God had more in store for them than walking the streets of a red-light district.

Just as I was struck by those smiles, the same thing happened when I went to Uganda. There I met lots of people and saw plenty of faces carrying the signs of potential. There were teenage boys who quickly and with masses of spirit and energy unpacked their dreams like a street vendor before a bunch of ambling tourists. There were yellow-eyed and toxic-breathed alcoholics whose age I never really could figure out. There were kids who only a short time before had cheated death on the streets and had undergone a soul transformation. All three types of young people, all works in progress, even the ones we'd assume had no hope.

I met Edward in a village of a thousand orphans and abandoned children. Sound depressing? Think again. The village is managed by an organization that thinks big yet does the details well. It is made up of clusters of small homes, each one managed by a "mother," a woman most likely widowed, abandoned or divorced, who pledges to bring up as her own the eight boys or girls living under her roof. Edward couldn't tell me much about his life before he was taken in as a baby, but he had plenty to say about the future.

"I will be an engineer. After I have graduated from university, I will work in England or America. Then I will come back to Uganda and build roads and schools and new villages like this."

I still have trouble coming up with any reason to doubt him. His confidence, ease around strangers, obvious affection for his family and deep-rooted love for others made him shine. Made him come alive. Made his faith strong. Surely the years will prove him right.

"Time and bad conditions do not favor beauty." I heard this around another village, one far away from the city, balanced 8,000 feet up on the top of a mountain. It described so many of the women, but many of them walked with unmistakable strength and grace.

The male population had their own troubles. Booze added an extra dimension of hardship to the lives of so many of the men. With boys only costing money rather than bringing in a dowry, and with no battles to fight or territories to defend, so many of the men I met had grown up absent of purpose. What else was there to do but drink and stare from the side of the road?

"Give me a job," one of the guys said to me.

"What could you do," my translator interrupted.

The others laughed at the silence that followed. I scanned the man's eyes for a sense that their joking was causing offence, but he was laughing harder than any of them. He thought it was funny that everyone had written him off. He thought he was finished and that it was all one big joke. But he had potential—so much God-given potential. It was just all too distant for him.

And then there was 13-year-old Justus. A year before I met him, he was living on the street, huffing glue and homebrew, trying to dodge those who wanted to practice their grim-reaper routine on these street kids whom they simply saw as "disposable assets." Then the English girl turned up.

Twenty-four years old, she had a head full of half hopes and vague plans and a heart too broken by the suffering to walk away. She took Justus in as her own, an instant odd couple playing house up the hill.

Just 10 minutes in their company was enough to overwhelm the cynic. Forget how it looked on paper, in the flesh and smiles and hugs and high fives, his was a life utterly transformed. It was not the greatness of the sacrifice that struck me—not the fact that the girl had taken the street kid in and decided to care for him into adulthood—it was its simplicity. She saw a problem, and she knew she could fix it. So she did.

Perhaps releasing the built-in potential God put in all of us isn't such a difficult process after all.

Perhaps it's not something that we need to leave to the experts.

Perhaps it's something for us all to consider.

Perhaps it's something that we can all do something with.

NOT ON OUR OWN

The same people who will tell you that suffering is the sign of failing faith might also want you to believe that greater things will happen as a result of our own skills. They're wrong again. We can do no great things, only small things with great love (God's kind). That's what a pint-sized nun in Calcutta once said, and she achieved the truly remarkable feat of bringing the care of the poor and the outcast to the attention of a world bent on consumption and greed.

No, we can do no great things ourselves. We can nothing to impress God. We can do nothing on our own to save the world. We have no great tricks up our sleeves.

Take a look at the Bible. There are any number of examples of characters falling into the trap of believing that they were marked out for greatness and that their own potential would help them get there.

Take Samson, for example. He was born at a time when the Israelites were locked in a repeating cycle of rebellion, judgment and deliverance. The nation was in dire straits, with God's people under the rule of the oppressive Philistine regime. Samson was born with a clear mandate: to free the Israelites and bring them back to God. And as the nation's future deliverer, there were some procedures in place for Samson to follow his entire life, the most well-known command being never to cut his hair.

It was quite a destiny for a young man, and the Bible takes time to reveal how he went about fulfilling it. Actually, that's not entirely true. The Bible takes time to reveal how Samson repeatedly messed up; how he lived according to his appetites rather than his sense of duty.

His early years were promising. We are told that Samson "grew and the LORD blessed him, and the Spirit of the LORD began to stir him" (Judg. 13:24-25). But things began to go wrong when Samson started to allow lust to rule his actions. Timnah was a small town about four miles away from Samson's home in Zorah. He fell in love with a Philistine woman there, but his decision to marry her was no-go. God had strict rules for the Israelites and who they could and could not marry—with so many violent enemies around, it was important that the Israelites remained Israelites through and through. But Samson had other ideas. He got nasty when his parents asked him whether he might prefer a nice Jewish girl instead. The answer, of course, was no. Actually, he yelled at his dad, saying, "Get her for me! She looks good to me" (Judg. 14:3, *NLT*).

Living so close to the town of Timnah and the territory of the Philistines is a prime picture of how Samson lived on the edge spiritually as well as physically. Samson pushed God's boundaries by breaking his rules for marriage. Later, at his wedding to the Philistine girl, Samson pushed the boundaries once more by provoking the Philistines. He told them a riddle and gave them seven days to figure it out. If they got it right he would give them 30 linen garments and 30 festal garments. If they failed, they'd give him the same things.

Okay, so a few threads might not seem like much, but these were serious outfits, the sort that a man might only expect to own one of during his entire lifetime. The fact that their failure would mean them having to hand over such a hefty prize was a pretty reasonable incentive to work the riddle out, and again Samson played with fire.

But what about the riddle, you ask? What's it all about? Well, it was all about the lion Samson had killed when it had attacked him and his parents a brief period earlier. With his bare hands and, more importantly, God's anointing, Samson tore the lion apart limb to limb. While God had saved him that day, at his wedding Samson was now using God's miracle to line his own pockets.

What happened next is baffling. On the fourth day, the Philistines conspired with his wife to trick him into giving her the answer so they would win the bet. They did. Facing bankruptcy because of his own stupidity, you'd imagine that God would give Samson the cold shoulder. But, no; Samson took a 30-mile hike to a coastal town called Ashkelon where he looted a village and killed 30 men, giving his booty to the Philistines to pay his debt. It's a horrific story, and it's made stranger by the fact that God helped him on this killing spree ("the Spirit of the LORD came upon him in power"; Judg. 14:19). Could God really be into killing 30 men? It's all confusing, yet somehow the lesson to learn from Samson's life becomes a little clearer when the story skips forward a bunch of years and covers his final, painfully tragic hours.

It is in this, Samson's final scene, that we find ourselves in the middle of one of the best Sunday School stories of all time.

Having been tempted and betrayed by Delilah (Samson was so annoyed at his wife for ratting out his answer to the riddle to the Philistines that his father gave her away to Samson's best man after the wedding; Delilah was just another Philistine woman he fell in love with), he found himself captive to the very people he was supposed to be rescuing the Israelites from. His strength gone and his eyes gouged out, Samson ended up in Gaza in the middle of a party the Philistines were having.

They asked for him to be brought in so he could entertain them. "Bring out Samson," the crowd cried. "He's good for a laugh." So Samson was wheeled out and chained between two columns in front of a crowd that was nicely lubricated on afternoon booze. And there he was: alone, frail and a pathetic laughingstock, such an oh-so-different picture from the glorious God-shaped vessel that was born for a specific purpose.

Yet in the same way that Samson's life was full of mess-ups followed by godly interventions, his death offers a few surprises too. He pushed the pillars apart and killed a whole load of people, himself included, but there's more to the story than that.

Judges 16:28 offers us the Bible's first and last record of Samson praying. That doesn't mean he didn't pray, but I suspect that the author could be trying to make a point: Samson, ever the man who followed his own agenda, is finally asking God for help. "Sovereign LORD, remember me again. O God, please strengthen me just one more time. With one blow let me pay back the Philistines for the loss of my two eyes" (Judg. 16:28, *NLT*). In asking God to strengthen him just one more time in order to avenge the loss of his sight, we get a clear indication that

Samson recognized that his strength came from God. Perhaps this is the truth he had waited his whole life to get.

It is impossible not to hear the sad tone of his story when his life ends. The Bible tells us that he "killed many more when he died than while he lived" (Judg. 16:30). Imagine what could have been if Samson had chosen to live his life God's way. Imagine where Samson's life could have led had he chosen to obey God. Samson's final days were spent blind, yet his whole life he lacked insight into his own behavior. He was unable to see that his habit of trusting in his own abilities and giving in to his own appetites was second best.

Perhaps there is more of Samson within us than we would like to admit. Perhaps we might not experience such an extreme range of highs and lows, but the theme of failing to live up to potential is one I know well. Samson's problem—and mine, maybe even yours—is not only the presence of sin but also the lack of basic understanding of just how this whole Christian life is supposed to pan out. I thought that my remarkably wonderful destiny as a revered preacher was a shoo-in, that it was a guarantee and that it would take nothing more than good PR on my part to bring it about. How wrong I was.

Samson's life contained moments of truly divine intervention when God's anointing resulted in remarkable acts. But they were God's divine interventions, works of grace rather than a result of personal sacrifice or integrity. Samson assumed that God's agenda was able to walk in step with his own. He couldn't have been more wrong. I don't know if I was ever on course for being an evangelist—and I sincerely suspect not—but I know that if it ever had happened, it would have had absolutely nothing to do with me.

SMALL STEPS TO GREAT THINGS

If Samson is an example of what not to do, then we need look no further than Jesus for a better alternative. The plot starts out the same, with two parents being made aware of the role their child will play in the future salvation of an oppressed people, but there the similarities end. Jesus, as well as being without sin, was also the living embodiment of living a life totally devoted to and in line with God's destiny. Not only that, but He taught us the importance of taking small steps to get there.

I once heard someone say, "Slow and steady wins the race." I think that's a pretty adequate picture of what happens when we partner with God in order to bring about greater things. We can't do everything at once. We can't start at the finish line. We can't begin our objectives with the end result. We have to, step by step, slowly and surely, follow God in His timing and in His will, starting with the small stuff.

This is what Jesus did. He wasn't even born with a bang. He didn't pop into the world as a warrior with His infant hand wrapped around the barrel of a gun. He grew up like a normal kid. He studied, He went to Temple, He was, as far as we can guess, a typical son and brother to His family. Even in the beginning of His public ministry, you don't see Him walking around town with a bullhorn, telling everyone who He was and what He planned to do. He met with and interacted with people all along the road toward Calvary. He had countless divine encounters with individuals of varying social standing whom He treated with equal love and compassion. No person was too insignificant, no task too lowly. There was no opportunity He would not take to inch forward His holy revolution.

Do you think we are destined for a holy revolution of our own? I mean, sure, it's okay for the Son of God to stir things up on a grand scale with simple acts, but can we really expect to do the same? Well, my friend, here's a secret . . . live a life, day by day, of small steps of obedience, sacrifice, justice, devotion, love and compassion, and you can't fail but end up being part of God's plan for the people and the planet. In other words, if you take it slow and steady, keeping integrity close and selfishness away, you'll end up like the tortoise that beat the hare.

GLORY SHINES

I've got a feeling that there are some other smiles buried deep within the sex workers of Pattaya. Smiles of hope, of promise, of healing, of deliverance. I believe that there has to be. God will intervene if we let Him. Through the pairing of human and divine justice, captives can be freed from their chains, whether the iron shackles are poverty, hunger, slavery, addiction, ignorance. But we must play our part and let God be God in our lives.

Yes, our world is one of suffering. Some is our own, some belongs to others. None of this is part of God's plan, but all of it can draw us closer to Him and to each other. And just like all that suffering, each of us is soaked in potential. At times we use it unwisely and make the story about ourselves; but at our best, when we follow Christ, we will find ourselves caught up in the essential work of God's kingdom, releasing that potential the way God intended.

There are greater things going on all around us. And there are more to come. But none of them are—or will be—the result of our own greatness or our own skill. By God's grace we'll be involved, a vehicle or a tool that He chooses to use, igniting further transformation in the world around us through the ultimate work of His hands.

None of it will be about us.

It will all be about Him.

The glory of God is not found in the achievements of His people. It's not revealed in the volume of the songs. It's not even held in the reputation of the Church. The glory of God is shown in lives transformed, in darkness overturned and in hope restored.

It is found in the smile of the redeemed, the prodigal welcomed with an embrace, and the woman at the well accepted. It is found wherever those who hear God's voice follow His instructions. It is found where people put aside their agendas and commit to loving and serving God and others. It is found in the small steps of constant devotion to the life and call of Jesus. It is found in the broken hearts that carry on loving, the weak hands that keep on serving, the joy released in the midst of sadness.

That's where the greater things reside.

That's where they get released.

And that, my friend, is where you belong.

AFTERWORD: GOD OF WHICH CITY?

Yours might be an actual city. It might be that you long to see God's glory shine through hearts alive with praise for Him in your town or the place where you took a mission trip last summer.

But you might not have an actual city in mind. It might be a school, a group of people, your church, an issue, even your own family. You might be drawn in by the gravity of a particular cause. Human trafficking has got under my skin, and I know that my compassion and will to act are getting fully engaged.

Whatever it is—a bricks-and-mortar city or a flesh-and-blood issue—find it. Name it. Move into it if you can, put your life on hold for a while if you must, pray with all the words you have and then into the silence. Spend the best of what you have to see transformation unleashed. Hold nothing back and let everything go in your reckless pursuit of God's simple—yet life-changing—command to love Him and love others as yourself.

Trust God to be there for you, but don't hand Him a map.

Stand firm, over time, with others and God.

Take small steps.

And smile.

ENDNOTES

One: Sweat

1. Anup Shah, "Poverty Facts and Stats," Global Issues, March 22, 2009. http://www glo balissues.org/article/26/poverty-facts-and-stats.
2. Shen Rujun and Royston Chan, "Over 33 Million Infected with AIDS Virus: U.N.," Reuters, November 24, 2009. http://www.reuters.com/article/idUSTRE5AN11 D20091124.
3. Megan Rowling, "World's Hungry Exceed 1 Billion, U.N. Tells *Financial Times*," Reuters AlertNet, March 27, 2009. http://www.alertnet.org/db/an_art/20316/2009/ 02/27-170057-1.htm.
4. "Water a Public Good?" UNEP, http://www.grid.unep.ch/product/publication/ freshwater_europe/consumption.php; Nancy L. Barber, "Summary of Estimated Water Use in the United States in 2005," USGS, http://pubs.usgs.gov/fs/2009/ 3098/.
5. "Three Children Die Each Minute from Infected Water, Says U.N.," EuropaWorld, January 4, 2005. http://www.europaworld.org/week217/three1405.htm.
6. Maria Colenso, "How Much Power Does the World Consume?" How Stuff Works. http://science.howstuffworks.com/world-power-consumption.htm.
7. "Forced Labor," ILO. http://www.ilo.org/global/Themes/Forced_Labour/lang— en/index.htm.
8. "Facts About Human Trafficking," U.S. Department of State. http://74.125.155.132/ search?q=cache:Px7csG3T8qoJ:www.state.gov/documents/organization/33216.pdf +us+state+department+trafficking+600,000&cd=1&hl=en&ct=clnk&gl=us&client= firefox-a.

Two: Us?

1. Rosemary Bennett and Ruth Gledhill, "Childcare Children Pay Price as Adults Put Themselves First," *The Times,* February 2, 2009. http://women.timesonline.co.uk/ tol/life_and_style/women/families/article5636038.ece.
2. Eugene Peterson, *The Gift: Reflections on Christian Ministry* (Grand Rapids, MI: Zondervan, 1995), p. 64.

Three: History

1. Dr. Martin Luther King, Jr., *Letter from a Birmingham Jail,* April 16, 1963, Birmingham, Alabama.
2. Ibid.
3. "The Problem Today," Stop the Traffik. http://www.stopthetraffik.org/human trafficking/problem.aspx.
4. "Declaration of the Rights of the Child," Resolution 1386 (XIV), adopted by the UN General Assembly on December 10, 1959. http://www.un.org/cyberschoolbus/ humanrights/resources/child.asp.

Five: Signs That Point to God

1. Rabbi Lawrence Kushner, *Jewish Spirituality: A Brief Introduction for Christians* (Woodstock, VT: Jewish Lights Publishing, 2001).

End child sex exploitation.

StandOut International
Information Pack

1 Belmont Office Park
232-240 Belmont Road
Belfast, Ireland BT4 2AW

Every dot here represents a child trafficked for sexual exploitation today. Just today alone.

2 children are trafficked for sexual exploitation every minute.

End child sex exploitation.

Introduction

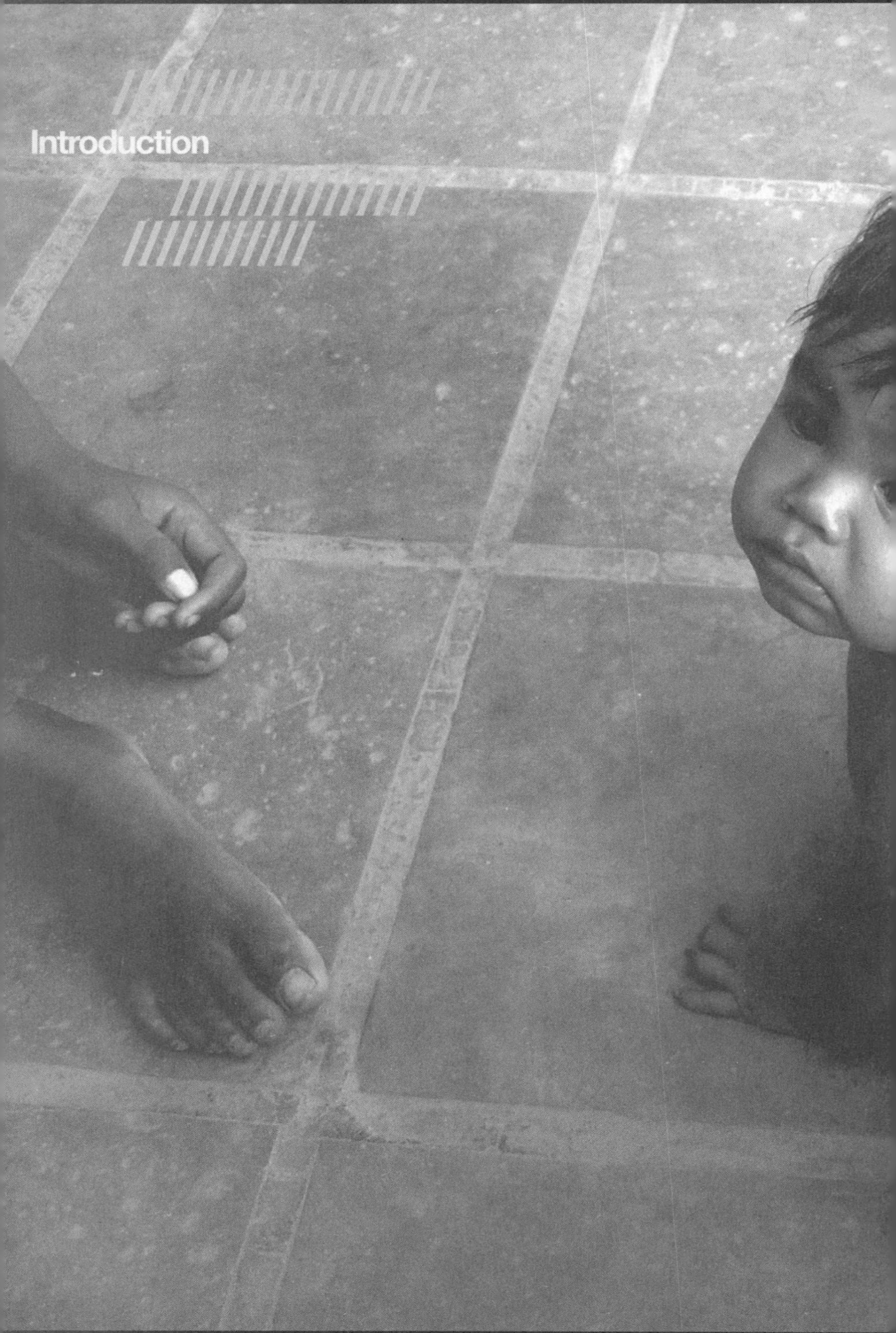

Worship.
Music.
Justice.

StandOut International is a Northern Ireland based non-profit organisation that fundamentally builds upon the platform of worship, music, justice. We exist to end child sex exploitation on a global scale whilst loving, educating and releasing those rescued into the fullness of life that God has for them.

What is child trafficking?
Child Trafficking is when children are deceived or taken against their will, bought, sold and transported into slavery for sexual exploitation, sold as child brides and used for sacrificial worship.

StandOut International believes that when people worship they encounter the genuine heart of God for all humanity. From His platform of love we are compelled to serve the needs of others and we ultimately become a voice for those who have no voice.

How it all began

It was in Thailand in Pattaya - a city scarred and stained by its reputation as the capital of the world's sex trade – that the story began…

"Growing up in Belfast means that we've grown used to people crying in church, begging God to change our city. I don't know whether you become numb to it all, but I do know that I had never really had those kinds of feelings for a particular place. It all changed that night in Pattaya. The feelings of compassion took over and I started just to sing out what I knew was true about who God is to the people of the city. And that was when it felt like things started to happen

The band had bartered their way into 'playing' at a club – a club above a brothel. As they did what they only ever do – worshipped – something arrived. It was a song – but one that formed with unusual power and speed. Lyrics and melody formed, calling out a message of hope, a promise of new life for a city so chained by darkness".

God Of This City: beyond the song

Aaron Boyd of Bluetree continues…
"I remember looking over to my left and seeing a group of English guys in the street. My guess is that they were just over to buy time with cheap Thai girls and do whatever they wanted with them.

But you could see their surprise as they heard the truth deep in the words we were singing out; that God was a part of this place, that greater things were to come, that there is a light that eliminates the darkness.

Something was happening, but whether it was in us or beyond us we couldn't tell. All we knew was that we'd been in the middle of something we'd not experienced before.

There's one part of the song that came along after the night:

'Where glory shines from hearts aloud with praise for you and love for you in this city…'

I picture those girls who are being sold on the street whenever I sing these words; girls that are perhaps more gorgeous than any you'll ever see, girls who smile at you and try their best to entice you in, girls whose lives are caught up in so much pain. But I'm convinced that they've got a better song to sing, I'm convinced that there's glory and praise that can shine from their hearts and lives.

But for us there's more to the song than the big names that have heard or liked it. As a band we just want to be obedient to whatever God's put in front of us and since God's blessed us with a song that's shouting across the world we've got some new opportunities ahead.

Off the back of it all – the touring, the sales and royalties – we're going to be able to support a number of different projects that help transform lives that would otherwise be trapped.

I believe the song is so powerful because it speaks the truth and it's truth that changes people's lives, that sets us free.

We – the Church – must be the source of love where there is no love. We should worry less about condemning the things that are wrong with the world, and put more of our energies in to putting those things right. We need to be the church that deals in love, not in hate. And we're called to do all this with the knowledge that greater, and greater and greater things are still to come.

We could sit and beg God to change India, Pattaya, Cambodia or whatever other oppressive situation you could mention, but I don't think that's the point: I don't think it's up to us to twist God's arm into fighting injustice, I think it's up to us to get on and fight it ourselves, to look around and realise quite how well God has equipped us to transform our communities and global neighbours.

That's what the song's all about, and that's why the stories that grow from it will be told by people we may never hear of – everyday Christians putting their faith into action and transforming their world, one person at a time".

Child Trafficking is an ugly thing. It makes for snappy headlines with heartstring-tugging stories.
But, the truth of child trafficking in Cambodia is complex. Most of the children in Riverkids would rather be sold to support their family than lose their family.

Families need support to care for their children, and some families need to le to care for their children. Stopping trafficking before it destroys childre lives is not easy. But it is alot easier than recovery for a child sold and lo.

Out of a determination to make a difference for the voiceless in Thailand and in other scenes of exploitation around the world, StandOut International was born.

Our aim is to raise awareness and channel funds through organisations like Viva who are active on the ground making a difference to children's lives every day.

We are called to be the hands and feet of Jesus, let's together stand out and make a difference.

You can be involved in many ways by:

- Financial Giving
- Prayer
- Volunteering
- Short term mission trips
- Organising events to raise awareness and support

"I looked for a man among them who would build up the wall and stand before me in the gap on behalf of the land... (Ezekiel 22:30 – NIV)

together for children

Viva's aim is to encourage and enable the Christian community to work together for the vulnerable children of the world.

Millions of children across the globe are growing up hungry, hurting, and without a home. Many Christians are responding to this need with compassion and courage, yet they are often ill-equipped and overstretched, working in isolation. Instead of creating another body to try and meet the need, Viva seeks to combine and connect what already exists, strengthening and uniting children at risk initiatives to release the enormous potential of a joint response. Viva has over 12 years of experience helping networks and projects care for children who have been exploited, malnourished, trafficked, abused, or abandoned. Viva currently supports more than 5,000 church-based projects through local networks, reaching over 1.3 million children around the world.

We are
called to
be the
hands
and feet
of Jesus

Ongoing projects

Daughters

The story so far...
There are children who live in brothels all over Cambodia. There are babies and small children who have not yet been sold into active prostitution but who experience abuse every day. They do not attend school and live every day exposed to the activities in the brothel. They will have few options for work outside of the brothel unless an intervention occurs. These young boys and girls are either the children of sex workers or children the brothel owner has acquired for selling later on. Most boys who have grown up in the brothels we work with end up becoming pimps and have drug addictions.

Looking to the future...
1. To provide a night shelter for the kids, to enable them to live in a safe, supportive and loving environment conducive to the healthy raising of children rather than in the brothel.

2. To provide comprehensive medical and therapeutic treatment to the kids.

Destiny Rescue Girl's Homes

The story so far...
The Destiny Rescue Girls' Homes in Cambodia have been operational in Kampong Cham since April 2006. A need arose in Kampong Cham following the closure of a well respected NGO that cared for sexually exploited girls.

Destiny Rescue had access to the community by way of an existing home for orphan children, and the first premises was rented and 4 staff hired. We also had experienced staff come from Australia to set up this project and to develop its potential. Two months later we had our first 5 girls arrive from an Assessment Centre.

Soon after that an independent assessment was made of the facilities and programs that we provided. Some recommendations were adopted and our reputation for quality care was placed on the map in Cambodia.

At a glance...
1. Girls live in four different homes, depending on their needs. Homes provide all food and clothing, plus at least one holiday each year, medical care 24 hours a day, and counseling services.

2. Formal and informal education on site, grades 1 to 7, plus creative arts education, e.g. photography, music, traditional and modern dance.

3. Daily spiritual expression in worship.

4. Awareness education on road safety, first aid, sexual exploitation, AIDS, relationships, self-esteem and numerous other pertinent subjects.

5. A reintegration team that unites families with their daughters where possible.

6. Community education, particularly in the areas of non judgmental approach with victims of child sexual exploitation.

Looking to the future...
1. Qualified counselors.

2. More residential rental properties to meet demand especially for long term girls unable to return to their homes.

3. Establish a restaurant in this town to train our girls and to provide income for them. We believe in self sustainability.

4. Develop a rural centre where girls can live and train.

5. How Can You Help?

Send me back for more.

StandOut)
International
Worship. Music. Justice.

Dear stand out international
I would like to (tick as appropriate)

☐ Become a prayer partner – please send me up-to-date information

☐ Talk to my friends / colleagues / church about StandOut – send me information to help with this

My details

Name:

Address:

Mobile number:

Email:

Send to:
StandOut International
1 Belmont Office Park
232-240 Belmont Road
Belfast, BT4 2AW

12 |

Greater
things have
yet to come.
Greater things
are still to
be done...
in this city

End child sex exploitation.

Stand Out)
International
Worship. Music. Justice.

1 Belmont Office Park
232-240 Belmont Road
Belfast, BT4 2AW

creative www.madebybreak.com

NEW ALBUM 'GREATER THINGS' OUT NOW

FOR MORE INFORMATION ABOUT BLUETREE AND
STANDOUT INTERNATIONAL, VISIT

WWW.GIVMUSIC.COM/BLUETREE

WWW.MYSPACE.COM/BLUETREEONLINE

WWW.STANDOUTINTERNATIONAL.CO.UK

WWW.FACEBOOK.COM/PAGES/STAND-OUT-INTERNATIONAL/149064605144

WWW.VIVA.ORG

CONTACT AARON BOYD AT
STANDOUT@VIVA.ORG

BLUETREE USES VESPER GUITARS
WWW.VESPERGUITARS.COM

Greater Things Have Yet To Come.

luetree is the inspired, creative trength behind the amazing new ong, *God Of This City*... A new hurch anthem for the world to eep it's head in the clouds but its eart in the streets.

Martin Smith [Delirious?]

.Having a missional mindset is ow Bluetree gives substance to hat they sing about... Bluetree is itentional about directing their ttention outwards.

Worship Leader Magazine

bluetree

Family Christian Store Exclusive

GOD OF THIS CITY
The Debut Album From **BLUETREE**
Available In Stores Nationwide And Online

Management: Tony Patoto & Andy Toogood / Fuel Music Management   management@bluetreeonline.co.uk
www.BluetreeOnline.co.uk   www.GivMusic.com/Bluetree

More Great Resources from
Regal Books

Sub-Merge
John B. Hayes
ISBN 978.08307.43063
ISBN 08307.43065

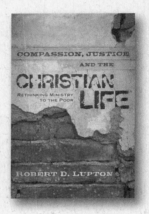

**Compassion, Justice
and the Christian Life**
Robert D. Lupton
ISBN 978.08307.43797
ISBN 08307.43790

Hands & Feet
Audio Adrenaline
ISBN 978.08307.39325
ISBN 08307.39327

With Justice for All
John Perkins
ISBN 978.08307.44954
ISBN 08307.44959

Regal
God's Word for Your World™
www.regalbooks.com

Available at Bookstores Everywhere!